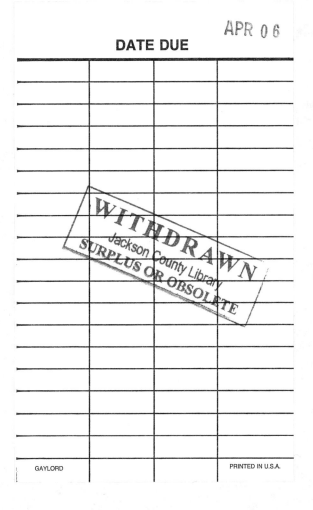

Cooking with Spirit
NORTH AMERICAN INDIAN
FOOD AND FACT

by Darcy Williamson
and Lisa Railsback

— A Maverick Publication —

Copyright © 1988 by Darcy Williamson

ISBN 0-89288-164-X

Maverick Publications
Drawer 5007 - Bend, Oregon 97701

CHAPTERS OF CONTENT

Introduction

To some, North American Indian cooking seems bland—unseasoned. The ingredients lack interest, and in many cases, appeal. But the native cooks of this country used what was at hand and took care to conserve their food sources so that there would always be plenty of generations which followed. They did not eat for sheer pleasure; they ate to survive, they ate what the land offered, and they seasoned their food with spirit.

The native plants, fish, and game were warrior foods, for they were the survivors of the fittest, the weaker foods having died off. Warrior foods made one strong, and strength meant a greater chance of survival for the Indians. When the people were forced onto reservations and fed government rations, they believed that they would become weak from the "new foods," which included "kept" meats —animals which were unclean from lack of activity.

Even with the drastic changes in environment and lifestyles, the North American Indians have undergone, attitudes in preparation of foods and choice of utensils remains important. As is traditional, foods are acquired with reverence and attention to its importance in the balance of nature. Each animal, fish or plant has unique qualities and powers, and are considered a relative to all life. When any are eaten, used or worn, these qualities become part of the person utilizing them. Even utensils, weapons and tools are channels of spirit energy, positive or negative, which can be passed to foods and material goods.

Harmony with nature is always important. Water flows clockwise and one must stir food in a clockwise direction. To flow with nature is survival. To remember that all life, plant and animal, should be regarded with reverence, is survival.

The attitude of persons preparing food is extremely important, also. A happy, peaceful cook is healthful, while anger or negative feelings cause inferior foods or illness. Love of one's family means joy in cooking.

Chapter I

Northwest Coast Culture Area

The Northwest Coast Culture area extends along the coast of northwestern America from Trinidad Bay in northern California to Yakutat Bay, Alaska. Tribes included in this area are the Tlingit, Haida, Tsimshian, Bella Coola, Kwakuitl, Nooka, Coast Salish, Chinook, Yurok and Hupa.

Fish is the staple food of the Northwest Coast tribes. Salmon, halibut, smelt, herring, cod and candlefish are favorites. Shellfish, such as clams, mussels, abalones, limpets, periwinkles, crabs and sea urchins are also popular. Seals, sea lions, porpoises, whales, duck, deer and black bear are hunted. Vegetable foods are less important. Those favored are arrowhead, seaweed, camas, acorns and unfurled ferns. Berries are abundant in this area and include salal, cranberries, blackberries, salmon berries, blueberries, huckleberries and blackcaps.

Traditionally, the three methods most often used in cooking were boiling, steaming and broiling. Watertight baskets or cedar boxes were used in boiling. Heated stones were placed in liquid, which had been poured in a watertight container. Within minutes, the liquid would begin boiling, and the foods contained in the liquid cooked quickly.

Steaming was done in shallow pits. The pit was filled with hot stones. Food was placed on top of the stones and covered with leaves, woven grass and rush mats. Water was poured through the stones, steaming the foods.

Fish and meat were often broiled over an open fire or over a bed of coals.

At meal time, long feast mats were unrolled to serve as tablecloths.

Arrowhead

Arrowhead Pickles (Modern)

2 quarts of arrowhead tubers
3 small red peppers, seeded
1 quart cider vinegar
½ cup brown sugar
¼ cup salt

Clean tubers. Pack whole in three sterilized one-quart jars. Add one red pepper to each jar. Mix vinegar, brown sugar and salt in pan. Bring to boil and simmer 5 minutes. Pour over arrowhead, filling jars to within ¼-inch of the top. Seal tightly. Ready to use in two weeks.

Tule Potatoes (Traditional)

Tule potatoes are often called arrowhead (Sagittaria). The tubers are found at the end of the long roots of this aquatic plant. Indians use their toes or long sticks to dislodge tubers. July to September is the harvest season.

Dig a small pit and line it with stones. Build a fire in the pit and burn until a good amount of coals have accumulated. Make a well in center of the coals and add the tubers. Rake coals over tubers and allow them to roast 45 minutes to an hour, or until tender. Peel and eat.

A tea made from the roasted and ground dandelion, gathered during an autumn night, is used as a cleansing tonic for the liver and gall bladder.

Bear Paws (Modern)

2 lbs. skinned bear paws
1 quart cider vinegar
Myrtle leaves
8 strips of bacon
2 onions chopped
2 carrots, sliced
3½ cups meat stock
1 cup dried serviceberries or salal berries

Marinate paws in vinegar and myrtle for 5 days. In Dutch oven, add bacon, onion and carrots. Cook until bacon is partially crisp. Add bear paws, stock and water to cover meat. Cover Dutch oven and simmer 8 hours. Add berries last half-hour of cooking.

Tlingit, Tsimshian and neighboring tribes made cooking boxes. These were formed from thin, cedar boards, wetted and steamed, then bent around partial cuts to form square-cornered, watertight vessels. These boxes were filled with water. Hot rocks were placed in the boxes along with fish or meat, and liquid. By replacing the rocks as they began to cool, steady boiling could be maintained.

Beaver Stew (Modern)

1 beaver, skinned and gutted
1 part candlefish oil
1 part cider vinegar
1 part water
Bundle of herbs
1 cup honey

Cut up beaver and throw it in a crock with a mixture of oil, vinegar, water, herbs and honey. Let stand for five days, then simmer in marinade for 4 hours over low heat. Add some onions and potatoes, if you like.

Fish, salmon and whales were the buffalo of the tribes of the Northwest Coast Culture Area. Seaweed, tubers and berries were their corn; and huge sea-going cedar canoes were their horses.

Why the Salmon is Respected

Once the son of a respected woman took a piece of salmon from the food box without permission. After being scolded, the boy went up river where he sat down and sulked. A voice called to him for a canoe, "Get in!" And in he climbed.

The canoe went further up river and came to a village with large houses. The front of the first house was painted with the "Qunis," or dog salmon design. Other fine house fronts were painted with the coho, sockeye, steelhead, and spring salmon. In front of the spring salmon house, the mysterious canoe ran ashore, and the people entered, the boy following.

"You are in the house of the Salmon People," Mouse Woman said, "you healed the crippled leg of the salmon chief when you took the fish from you mother's food box. The chief's leg was cured because you straightened the salmon."

Of course, the boy was baffled at what Mouse Woman told him.

"The chief brought you here to be properly rewarded. But," the Mouse Woman warned, "eat none of the food offered, not even what looks like berries, because they are eyes of dead people!"

"But I am hungry," complained the boy, "what shall I eat?"

"Wait until tomorrow," Mouse Woman instructed, "then go outside where children, who are really salmon, will be playing. Catch a child, hit him with your club, and eat him. Then you must carefully burn every bone and all the salmon parts that you do not eat.

The boy discovered that the child became a real salmon the instant he clubbed it. Satisfying his hunger, the boy burned the bones and returned to the fine house. Suddenly, a child burst through the door screaming, "One of my eyes is gone!"

Instantly, Mouse Woman materialized. "You failed to burn one of the eyes of the salmon. Go find the eye and burn it! Hurry!"

When the boy did as instructed, he saw the child's eyes were normal again. Several days later, the salmon child sent the boy to see if the new leaves were on the trees. The seeds were their food. "Far up river the new leaves have budded," the boy reported.

"That is good," said the chief. "We go to the seed ground tomorrow."

A salmon skin was given to the boy. "Put this on for our journey," the chief ordered, "you will go with us."

Diving into the water, the boy discovered the salmon skin enabled him to swim as fast as a salmon. In fact, the young man became a salmon, and with the others, he swam upstream toward the spawning grounds.

"See what a huge Qunis I have caught!" shouted a chief, who was netting salmon in the rapids near his village. "This is the largest I have ever seen." He took the big salmon to his wife.

When she cut the great Qunis open with her clam shell knife to prepare the feast, she discovered a child in the salmon.

From this experience with the supernatural salmon, the people learned to ceremoniously burn all the bones and uneaten parts of the first salmon caught in the spring. Thus, the salmon spirits knew that the clan was respected and the ceremony became a great event and evolved into a "new year" ritual in which all of the nature spirits were involved to assure that all things would be renewed.

Bella Coola Dried Salmon *(Traditional)*

Heads and intestines were removed from the salmon. They were then split open and tied by their tales (often with whale sinew) to long, slender poles. Sticks are used to hold the salmon open. The poles were then elevated to approximately four feet above ground. Racks for holding the poles were often made and left in place at fishing grounds for another harvest. A fire was sometimes built beneath the rack and kept low. Green cedar bows were frequently placed on the coals. The sun and coals combined dried the fish in a week or two, depending on the weather. The dried fish was then rubbed with eulachon oil—a rich oil made from candlefish—before being stored for winter use.

Berry Bricks *(Traditional)*

Gather berries in season—salal, blackberries, wild strawberries, huckleberries. Mash berries together. Pour into a greased, rectangular wooden form to two inches thick and set in sun to dry. This takes seven days or longer, depending on temperature.

Remove dried berry brick and store in dry place for later use.

(Candlefish or whale oil was most commonly used to grease forms)

Broiled Duck *(Traditional)*

3 wild ducks, cleaned
Scant handful of sea salt

Rub ducks with salt, inside and out. Roast on green willow stick over open fire. Serve crackling crisp.

Chinook Berry Shortcake *(Modern)*

2 pints berries, such as wild strawberries,
  huckleberries, blackberries or a mixture
1 pint fresh cream
¼ cup sugar
2 cups flour
3 tsp. baking powder
2 Tbsp. sugar
¼ cup butter
1 egg
½ cup milk

Mash berries slightly; sprinkle with ¼ cup sugar and set aside. Sift together flour, baking powder and 2 Tbsp. sugar. Cut in butter until mixture resembles coarse cornmeal. Beat egg into milk. Stir this into dry ingredients, just to moisten. Knead dough gently, then roll to 1½ inches thick. Cut into 6 large squares. Bake on greased cookie sheet at 425-degrees F. 15 to 20 minutes.

Split shortcakes in half, pour some berries on bottom half. Replace top and pour some berries over all. Pass the milk.

Cooked Squashberries *(Traditional)*

Gather a quantity of squashberries and mash them; mix with candlefish oil, then fry the mass on a hot, flat stone. Eat while hot.

Many of the coastal tribes were, and remain skilled artists. They carve elaborate, wooden, spatula-like spoons which they use to eat sopalalli (soapberries, a very popular staple) made by whipping the crushed berries with water and candlefish oil until foamy.

The Tlingit, Haida and Tsimshian carved intricate patterns on mountain sheep horns, forming beautiful bowls, spoons and ladles.

Dulse-Shellfish Stew *(Modern)*

Dulse is a pinkish-red seaweed, which grows on submerged rocks, shells and ledges. This mineral-rich sea plant was and still is widely used by coastal tribes.

Gather a few handfuls of dulse and a basketful of shellfish, such as periwinkles, clams, mussels, shrimp or crab legs.

Sear dulse in skillet over campfire. Set aside. Bring kettle of water to boiling. Add a few myrtle or bay leaves, some chopped onion, celery and garlic. Toss in a handful of arrowhead tubers, camas, or small potatoes. Cook until nearly tender. Dump in shellfish and seared dulse. Cook 8 to 10 minutes. Ladle into bowls.

Dances were often held in relation to food. They placated evil spirits who brought devastating storms and supplicated the spirits controlling fish and game. Following a successful hunt, there were also dances to appease the spirit of the slain animal so that it would not take offense and make hunting difficult in the future.

Elk Stew with Acorn Dumplings *(Modern)*

4 pieces bacon, halved
1½ lb. cubed elk meat
1 quart water
1 onion, diced
1 tsp. salt
2 bay leaves
3 potatoes, diced
2 carrots, sliced
¼ cup ground acorn meal (recipe follows)
½ cup cold water

Dumplings
½ cup ground acorn meal (recipe follows)
½ cup whole wheat flour
1½ tsp. baking powder
2 Tbsp. milk
2 Tbsp. oil
1 egg, beaten

13

Squashberry

Brown meat with bacon. Add water, onion, salt and bay. Cover and simmer 1½ hours. Add potatoes and carrots and cook 30 minutes longer. Combine ¼ cup acorn meal with ½ cup water and stir into simmering stew.

In bowl, combine dumpling ingredients and beat until smooth. Drop by spoonfuls into simmering stew. Cover tightly and steam 12 to 15 minutes.

Acorn Meal *(Traditional)*

Shell acorns, then pound or grind them into meal. Place meal in basket with tight weave (or a cotton pillow case), but loose enough for water to pass through. Submerge basket in stream for two to three days. Stir the meal occasionally. The moving water will wash out the bitter tannin and leave the meal sweet. Remove basket from stream and let water drain free. Press meal into cakes, then dry in sun (or oven) for later use.

A tea made from the green bark of the oak is a powerful astringent and antidiarrhetic. It is also used as a cure for bad smelling feet.

How Eel Lost his Bones and Scales

One day Eel and Suckerfish challenged each other to the ancient gambling stick game.

"I'm an expert in the stick game," said the Eel.

"You needn't look far to meet your match," said the Suckerfish.

They played the whole night. In the end, Suckerfish defeated Eel. He won from him everything he had, even his scales.

Eel said, "I'm going to bet my bones on another game." So they played more of the stick game. By the time the sun rose, Eel had lost all his bones.

This is why Eel had no scales or bones. He lost them to the Suckerfish.

Thus, the eel is slimy, boneless and easily eaten, whereas, the suckerfish has numerous bones and scales and is difficult to eat.

Columbia River Eel *(Modern)*

2 lbs. eels, sliced or cut-up
1 lb. thick, sliced tomatoes
1 bunch green onions, chopped
1 lb. mushrooms, chopped
Salt and pepper
Lard or fat

Cover bottom of baking pan or dish with half the mixture of tomatoes, onions and mushrooms. Put eel over this and cover with other half of vegetable mixture. Add a few tablespoonsful of lard or fat and bake at 350-degrees F. for 35 to 40 minutes.

The Haida relish a grease from the hair seal. These natives carve beautiful, hardwood oil dishes, often in the shape of the seal. These dishes hold the coveted grease in which the Haida dip their foods.

Haida Fried Clams *(Modern)*

4 dozen medium clams, shelled
2 cups cornmeal
4 eggs, beaten
1 cup milk
4 cups oil for deep-frying

Dip clams in cornmeal, then in mixture of beaten eggs and milk and again in cornmeal. Fry in deep, hot fat, preheated to 385-degrees F., until golden brown. Drain on absorbent paper.

High Bush Cranberry Jelly *(Modern)*

Pick ripe bush berries from the stem and put them in a stone jar. Set the jar in a cast iron kettle, and let the fruit boil until the juice is extracted. Pour into a flannel bag or pillow case and let it drip through without squeezing.

To each pint of juice, add one pound of white sugar. Boil twenty to thirty minutes and keep it well skimmed. Put in the glasses while hot, seal with wax and sun daily until jellied.

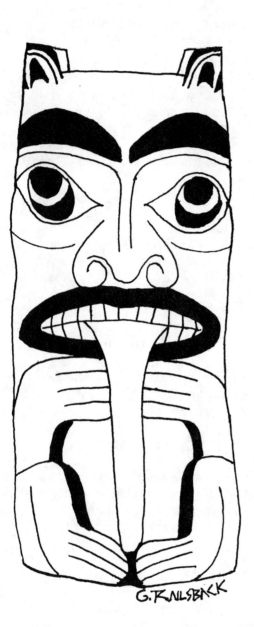

G. RALSBACK

The Tlingit and several other Northwestern Coastal Tribes made special halibut hooks of hardwood, shaped like a "V," with a short arm and a bone fastened to the short side. The shafts of these hooks were carved with figures which had magic powers. Two hooks were attached by short lines to the ends of the cross-pole. A sinker was attached to the center. The cross-pole held the buoyant, wooden hooks clear of the line.

Hupa Halibut with Sea Bird Eggs

(Traditional)

Put water in water-tight basket or cedar box, place heated stones in container and make water boil. Add halibut, cut up some. Drain off water and cut halibut up finely. Throw away bones. To basket with halibut, add six to eight sea bird eggs and beat up. Add some candlefish oil. Add more hot rocks to halibut and sea bird eggs until cooked up.

An Old Telling:

During the creation, everything was filled with life. Every tree, plant, mountain, plateau and river had spirits, and all creatures could communicate with one another. Land, sea and air creatures conversed with men, and their spirits were of equal vitality. All the animals could remove their fur or feather coats, enabling each to perform many acts of magic. In some regions, the ancient traditions tell of the time when fire spirits were selfish and would not help the people obtain fire with which to cook and warm their lodges. Similarly, the spirits controlling rain had to be dealt with, and magic gradually evolved into Shamanism.

Hupa Octupus Friters *(Modern)*

3 lbs. octopus, cleaned
1 tsp. salt.
1/3 cup cooking oil
2 minced green onions
2 eggs
1 cup unbleached flour

16

Drop octopus in kettle of rapidly boiling water and cook for 20 minutes. Drain and plunge in ice water. Scrape off purple skin. Discard head. Chop meat fine. Mix with onion, eggs and flour. Shape into flat cakes and brown in hot oil in skillet. Serve with butter and lemon, if desired.

Kwakuitl Potato Salad *(Modern)*

> 6 medium potatoes, boiled and peeled
> 1 onion, peeled and diced
> 2 cups fiddlehead ferns, steamed tender crisp and diced
> 6 hard-cooked eggs, peeled and diced
> 1 cup diced celery
> ½ cup cider vinegar
> 1 Tbsp. honey
> ¼ tsp. celery seed
> 1 Tbsp. mustard
> 1 cup mayonnaise
> Salt and pepper

Mix together vinegar, honey and celery seed. Pour over steamed ferns and allow to stand 3 hours. Combine potatoes, onion, eggs and celery. Mix together mayonnaise and mustard. Stir fern mixture into potato mixture and blend gently. Season to taste.

Kwakuitl Steamed Potatoes *(Traditional)*

The Kwakuitl people have planted potato patches since early historic times—the alkaline soil of their homeland seemed well adapted to this crop.

Dig a shallow pit and fill with hot stones. Lay dried grasses over stones, then place tubers on grass. Cover with more layers of grass to about a 3 inch thickness. Slowly pour a little water through the layers of grass and allow to steam. After an hour, pour another small quantity of water over grass. Uncover pit an hour later. Potatoes will have steamed to perfection.

Basketry

Tlingit and Haida basketry could be finely or tightly woven so as to make water-tight for cooking or loose weave for storing dried foods. These were made from cedar bark and spruce root. Decorative patterns (false embroidery) was done in bleached and dyed grasses. Cedar root was used for its rigid strength and resistance to salt water rot in open-work baskets for collecting shellfish, smelt, candlefish, and other sea creatures where drainage was desirable. When collecting shellfish the baskets were emersed in water and shaken so that sand washed from the shells.

Laver-Seafood Soup *(Traditional)*

Gather laver during low tides of May and early June. Lay the seaweed in the sun. Turn frequently until laver has thoroughly dried. Chop and crumble into pieces. Keep dry until needed.

To prepare soup, soak dried laver in water for 1 to 1½ hours. Add one cup of soaked laver to 2 cups water in water-tight basket. Drop in a hot stone or two. When the stones cool, remove and replace with another hot one. After soup has been boiling for 15 to 20 minutes, toss in chunks of fish, limpets, sea urchins, squid or other seafood which has been gathered. Cook until seafood is ready to eat (10 to 15 minutes).

Lillie's Huckleberry Jam *(Modern)*

> 4 cups crushed huckleberries
> Juice of 1 lemon
> 1 pkg. powdered pectin
> 5 cups sugar

Mix berries, juice and pectin. Bring to hard boil over high heat one minute, then add sugar and boil hard one minute longer. Remove from heat and stir and skim. Pour into jelly glasses and seal with paraffin.

Mussels *(Modern)*

> 3 dozen Pacific mussels
> Water
> Juice of 1 lemon
> ½ cup butter, melted

In saucepan, add 2 inches of water. Add mussels, cover and steam 3 minutes. Cool and remove shells. Serve with melted butter mixed with lemon juice.

17

Highbush Cranberry

Indians from the Northwest Coast Culture area used salal berries, which grow in great quantities along the Pacific Coast. The dark, plump, soft berries reach their peak in late August. The natives mashed the berries and dried the pulp on mats of skunk cabbage leaves. The dried pulp was then pelled off, rolled up and stored for winter use. It was often served with a smearing of candlefish oil. This delicacy is still served during special celebrations.

Nightwalker's Freezer Jam *(Modern)*

4 cups mashed salal berries
6 cups sugar
1 pkg. pectin
1 cup water

Stir together fruit and sugar and allow to stand for 1 hour.

Boil together pectin and water, stirring constantly, 1 minute. Add to berry mixture. Pour into clean jars, cover with cheese cloth and let stand 48 hours. Seal with lids and freeze until ready to use.

Pigweed *(Traditional)*

The young plants are eaten raw or cooked as a potherb. The seeds are shaken out on a clean, flat surface. They are consumed raw or ground into a meal. The meal can be mixed with equal parts of corn meal and made into a gruel.

The Nootka were skilled whale hunters. They would first harpoon the whale from a frail canoe, then attach sealskin floats so that the whale could not dive below the water's surface. Many times the small craft was towed along for days before lances killed the whale. Often brave Nootka would leap onto the whale's back and spear it to death. A successful hunt provided flesh and skin for food, intestines for oil containers, and sinew for rope. None was wasted.

Nootka Poached Salmon *(Modern)*

5-lb. fresh salmon, cleaned with head and
  tail removed
2 onions, chopped
2 celery stalks
2 carrots, scraped
2 bay leaves
1 tsp. salt

Put fish in a large roasting pan. Put half of the chopped onions in the cavity and the remainder around the fish. Place celery and carrots on fish. Add bay and salt, plus sufficient water to cover fish. Bake at 400-degrees F. for 15 minutes, then 350-degrees, covered, for 30 minutes.

"...I am sad for all the Indian people throughout the land.

"For I have known you when your forests were mine, when they gave me my meat and my clothing...But in the long hundred years since the white man came, I have seen my freedom disappear like the salmon going mysteriously out to sea..."—Chief Dan George, Salish Chief, 1967

Roasted Pacific Woodcock *(Traditional)*

4 woodcocks
Small handful of sea salt
Candlefish oil

Rub woodcocks inside and out with salt and candlefish oil. Roast over fire until tender inside but crisp outside. As birds roast, add additional oil and salt, brushed on with a green branch.

Ruby's Oyster Soup *(Modern)*

Take 2 quarts oysters, wash them and add 2 quarts water, a bundle of herbs, a small onion, sliced, and let it boil until all substance is out of the oysters. Strain the liquid from the ingredients and pour it back in the pot. Add a big spoonful of butter mixed with flour. Remove oysters from shells and add to this liquid mixture. Stir up two egg yolks with a cup of cream and cook it up in the pot. Don't let soup boil.

19

Salal

The Haida made elaborately carved, hardwood clubs about 15 inches long. These were used to kill hooked halibut and harpooned seals.

Sea Urchin Eggs *(Traditional)*

Gather only urchins from the temperate and arctic waters at low tide. Split the thin, fragile shells in half. The length of eggs inside the top shell are edible both raw and cooked.

"When the tide is out, the table is set."

Shellfish Bake *(Traditional)*

Dig a pit in the sand 4-ft. deep and 4-ft. wide. Line the pit with stones and build a large fire on stones and burn hot for four to five hours. When coals have well-heated the rocks, brush the coals aside. Cover stones with a 4-inch layer of rock-weed or seaweed. Lay shellfish on seaweed layer—clams, chunks of seal, crabs, mussels, limpets, periwinkles, sea urchins. Cover seafood with a 6-inch layer of seaweed. Lay branches or brush on top of the seaweed to hold in steam. The steam will have cooked the shellfish in an hour's time, but can be left as long as 2 hours in the pit without drying out.

The coastal tribes devised numerous methods of harvesting fish. The Kwakuitl built salmon traps of reed and stakes. A fence was built of these materials and extended some distance beyond the low-water banks of the river. Attached to the fence was a box-like structure located in the middle of the river. On each side of the box were two short frames with openings which led into long, narrow fish baskets.

All the coastal groups made dip nets fashioned of bags of netting attached to a wooden frame with a handle. They were used for netting salmon, herring and smelt.

Larger nets were made for gill-netting, often being fashioned into huge bags for trawling from canoes. This method was particularly popular among the Coast Salish and groups southward.

Harpoons of various designs were used. The northern-most group used harpoons with a single, one-piece, barbed bone or horn tip. From the Kwakuitl territory to northwestern California, two-pronged harpoons were used.

Short, light harpoons were made for throwing at salmon swimming in shallow water.

Angling was also a successful method used by tribes. The hooks were formed from straight, wooden shafts, to which a bone or horn point had been lashed at an acute angle. These hooks were attached to a hand line.

Other fishing devices included herring rakes and sharp flounder sticks.

Smoked Herring *(Modern)*

Clean and gut herring, leaving head on. Rub with a mixture of:

1 lb. coarse salt
2 cups brown sugar
1 Tbsp. salt peter
2 Tbsp. garlic powder
1 Tbsp. whole cloves, crushed
1 Tbsp. crushed bay or myrtle leaves
2 Tbsp. onion powder

Let herring cure in mixture for 7 days at 35 degrees F. Reapply mixture when needed, so that fish always remains fully coated.

After seven days, rinse in fresh water and hang up until thoroughly dried. Smoke at 70 to 85 degrees F. in home smoker for 7 days. Will keep refrigerated for one year or frozen for several years.

Thimbleberries and Salmon Eggs
(Traditional)

Gather thimbleberries after dew has left. Dry in sun. Mix with partially dried salmon eggs. A delicacy!

Pigweed

Steet-athls and A-sin *(Sasquatches)*

The Sasquatches who visited the Salish tribes were believed to live in mountain caves. They skulked about at night and could only be discerned by placing a stick in a mound of damp soil. If the stick was knocked down during the night and no evidence of tracks, the "steet-athls" were known to have visited. Among the tribes of the northern Oregon coast, Sasquatch was believed to be the creator of the red huckleberries, which, if picked and eaten at night, caused insanity. The female, called A-sin, was fond of stealing children. Shamans, desiring to cause trouble, would dream of A-sin, and thus the Shamans gained the power to bewitch people.

Tlingit Dried Salmon with Berries

(Traditional)

> **Pounded dried salmon**
> **Dried berries**
> **Whale or candlefish oil**

Combine all mentioned into a paste by mashing. Can be stored for a long period of time.

Since the foods of the Northwest Coastal people were rich in oil, soft, shredded, cedar bark was used for napkins and aprons.

Tlingit Reed Birds *(Traditional)*

Skin a dozen or more reed birds. Pick open and remove insides. Place them between folds of a cedar bark mat, and with a stone, mash the bones quite flat. Sprinkle with candlefish oil, thread on green willow sticks and roast over a clean fire.

Indian women's spirit is put into the food she prepares. It is therefore, important that her attitude remains positive during preparation. Food is necessary for survival. Good spirit and attitude are pro-survival.

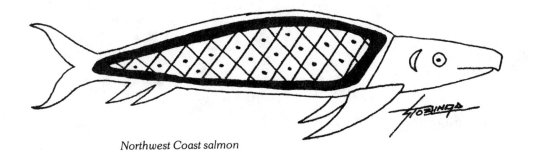

Northwest Coast salmon

23

Thimbleberry

Chapter II

California-Intermountain Culture Area

The California-Intermountain Culture Area includes California, Nevada, Utah, Idaho, the majority of Oregon, Washington and part of Canada. It extends eastward to the Rocky Mountains and encompasses the Great Basin and the Plateau. Tribes included in this area are the Paiute, Shoshone, Nez Perce, Flathead, Kutenai, Shuswap, Thompson, Wintun, Pomo, Maidu, Miwak, Yokuts, Cayuse, Yakima, Walla Walla and Umatilla.

These tribes were all native food gatherers, and did not practice agriculture. Tribes of the Great Basin relied on grass seeds and pinon nuts. Rabbits were the major game animal, but antelope were also hunted.

In the Plateau, roots, such as camas, were important. Berries were also a valuable food source. The Plateau people hunted elk, bighorn, caribou, deer, bear, rabbit, buffalo, fresh water fish and small game.

California tribes had an abundance of rabbits, deer and fish. Acorns were the main daily food of three-forths of the native Californians. The nuts were abundant, easily gathered and stored well. Baskets of nuts were often buried in the ground until needed. White acorns were the preferred, since they were the sweetest and were often eaten without leaching.

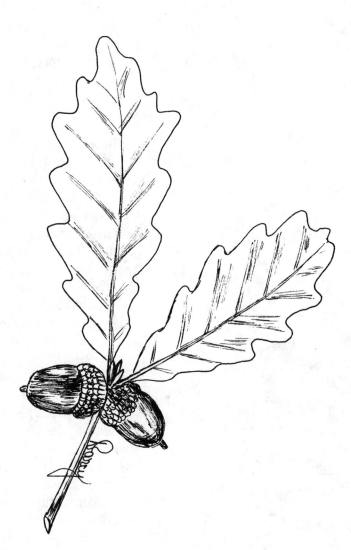

Oak

Acorn Bread *(Modern)*

6 Tbsp. cornmeal
½ cup cold water
1 cup boiling water
1 tsp. salt
1 Tbsp. butter
1 pkg. active dry yeast
¼ cup lukewarm water
1 cup mashed potatoes
2 cups all-purpose flour
2 cups finely ground leached acorn meal

Mix cornmeal with cold water, add boiling water and cook 2 minutes, stirring constantly. Add salt and butter and cool to lukewarm. Soften yeast in lukewarm water. Add remaining ingredients to corn mixture, along with yeast. Knead to a stiff dough. Dough will be sticky. Cover and let rise in warm place until doubled in bulk. Punch down, shape into two loaves, cover and let rise until doubled in bulk. Bake at 375-degrees F. for 45 minutes.

Acorn Meal

Shell acorns, then pound or grind them into meal. Place meal in basket with tight weave (or a cotton pillow case), but loose enough for water to pass through. Submerge basket in a stream for two to three days. Stir the meal occasionally. The moving water will wash out the bitter tannin and leave the meal sweet. Remove basket from the water and let water drain free. Press meal into cakes, then dry in sun.

"The white people never cared for land or deer or bear. When we Indians kill meat, we eat it all up. When we dig roots, we make little holes. We only shake down acorns and pinenuts—we don't chop down the tree." — Wintun woman

Acorn Griddle Cakes *(Modern)*

⅔ cup finely ground leached acorn meal
⅓ cup unbleached flour
1 tsp. baking powder
¼ tsp. salt
1 Tbsp. honey
1 egg, beaten
¾ cup milk
3 Tbsp. melted butter

Combine dry ingredients. Mix together egg and milk, then beat into dry ingredients, forming a smooth batter. Add butter. Drop batter onto hot, greased griddle. Bake, turning each cake when it is browned on underside and puffed and slightly set on top. Makes 12 to 15.

Acorn Gruel *(Traditional)*

Hull acorns and place in basket. Sprinkle with water. Allow basket to stand in shaded areas until mold forms on acorn meals (a couple of weeks to one month). Bury nuts in clean, fresh-water sand and leave them until they turn black (up to several months). Pound blackened acorns into meal.

To make gruel, add one part meal to two parts water and cook in basket by adding hot stones, one at a time, removing each stone as it cools. Mixture will boil and thicken. This gruel is eaten from the common basket, using fingers.

Bear Stew *(Modern)*

10 lbs. bear meat, trimmed of fat
Flour, salt and pepper
Fat
Wild onions, carrots and celery (including leaves)
6 to 8 cups bear stock, made from boiled bones

Cut meat into 1½-inch cubes, coat with flour mixture and brown in fat with onions. Add vegetables and stock. Simmer until tender.

Boxelder

Boxelder Syrup *(Traditional)*

The Boxelder is found throughout the states and the Rocky Mountains along streams in valleys and canyons.

Between the first day of the new year and the appearance of leaves in the spring, bore a hole on the sunny side of the trunk. Insert a hollow reed into the hole and let the sap flow into a bark vessel.

Boil the sap down in a container, using hot stones. Or, if during the cold season, allow the sap to freeze overnight and in the morning throw away the frozen water, leaving the syrup at the bottom of the container.

"The Great Spirit appointed the roots to feed the Indians on...The ground and water. The Great Spirit has given us our names. We have these names and hold these names. The ground says, The Great Spirit has placed me here to produce all that grows on me, trees and fruit. The same way the ground says, it was from me man was made. The Great Spirit, in placing men on the earth, desired them to take good care of the ground and do each other no harm..."—Young Chief of the Cayuse

Camas Bulb *The camas plant is botanically related to the hyacinth, and the edible bulb has a high-sugar content. They are best when cooked by roasting or steaming. Bulbs can be sun-dried for storage, after being flattened into cakes. As an important food source to the Northwest Indians, many wars were fought over meadows where the camas grew, for collecting rights.*

Harvest when camas is in bloom, as it is easier to distinguish edible camas from death camas—both grow in the same location. Edible camas has blue blossoms, whereas death camas has white.

Canadian Goose *(Traditional)*

1 large Canadian goose
Cooked high-bush cranberries
2 cups dried, chopped apples
14 juniper berries
Fat

Mix apples with berries and stuff goose with mixture. Rub fat all over bird and run a stick through bird. Suspend over slow fire and roast. With an elderberry or chokecherry branch, which has been frayed on one end, brush melted fat over bird.

When gathering flowers, leaves and stems, or roots of plants, a law of natural flow of sap (plant's blood) should be considered. The flow follows the daily path of Sun and Moon. As the sun rises and sets, so does the plant sap. Should the leaves and stems be needed, they can be taken in the morning or late afternoon. Flowers should be gathered between 11:00 and 2:00 p.m. Roots should always be gathered when Moon is high (at night).

These considerations will give maximum potency for medicinal use. Use care when harvesting the leaves and flowers, so as not to badly damage the plant. If the roots must be used, give an offering in honor of that plant. Never take more than will be needed. A plant Spirit will give its healing power only when appropriately addressed. Care and consideration is always good medicine.

Just as you are spirit, so are plants.

Cattail Shoots *Pull new sprouts early in spring by grasping tender inner leaves and pulling upward. Remove outer portion and cut off the top of the leaves. Eat the tender, innermost white stem, either raw or steamed.*

The root, made into a poultice and applied to sores, has good healing quallities.

Deer Liver *(Modern)*

1 deer liver, cut into slices
Wild onions, chopped
Sage, minced
Salt pork, chopped
Oil

Combine onions, sage and salt pork and spread a coating of the mixture on each slice of liver. Heat oil in heavy pan and gently cook liver, uncovered, for 25 to 30 minutes over low flame.

Camas

Keeping Game Fresh Hang meat in cool, dark place, wrapped with wet cloths, on top of which lay bows of elderberry to keep off insects. Keep meat as clean as possible so that it will not be necessary to wash it, since water extracts the natural juices.

Digger Steamed Clover (Traditional)

The Diggers were members of the Shoshone family and lived in an area where food was scarce. Steamed clover was a delicacy.

Dig a 2-ft. wide by 2-ft. deep pit. Build a fire on top of the stone layers. Usually juniper, pinyon or sage brush was used.

After stones are hot, brush coals away. Using forked sticks, remove one layer of rocks. Place clover (red or white) in water to thoroughly dampen. Place on hot rocks; place additional hot stones on top of wet clover. Cover all with juniper, pinyon or sage branches and allow to steam 30 to 40 minutes.

Digger Grasshopper Cakes (Traditional)

Since these Indians lived in such a harsh environment, where even wildlife could not thrive, they had to make use of what was available. Some years, grasshoppers were abundant. The Indians would dig a large, deep pit, then drive or herd the grasshoppers into the pit. The insects would be flailed to death with branches. The grasshoppers would then be gathered up and pounded into a pulp. This pulp would be compressed into cakes and dried in the sun.

Tea made from the root-bark of the elder relieves headache and mucus congestion.

Elderberries Gather berries after the first frost. Hang clusters and let them dry in the sun. Pick dried berries from the stems and store for winter use. Stew dried berries with honey or sap. Add a handful of dried berries to stews or soups. Work dried berries into a bread dough. The Indians found numerous uses for this dried fruit—they are similar to currants.

Dishes were sometimes made of mountain sheep horn which had been boiled, split and flattened. Split buffalo horn, fitted and sewn together with sinew, made a flaring dish. These dishes were used as eating plates.

Ember Roasted Tuber (Traditional)

Place tubers in hot coals, leaving a few coals to cover. Turn frequently until tender (approximately 20 minutes for small and 1 hour for large tubers).

This method can be used for camas, wild turnips, potatoes, etc.

There is no such thing as a weed to the Indian, for all plant life had its place and purpose in nature's balance.

Flixweed (Traditional)

Gather the seed heads from the flixweed. Pound the dry pods and winnow the seeds from the chaff. Parch the seeds on a hot stone, then grind them into a meal.

This meal is used cooked into mush, mixed with other meals to make bread, or used in thickening soups.

Fried Squirrel (Modern)

2 squirrels, cut into halves
Salt
Pepper
Flour
Lard
Water

Dredge squirrels with mixture of salt, pepper and flour. Fry in hot lard in skillet until golden. Drain off all but 2 Tbsp. lard. Bring 1½ cups of water to boiling and pour over squirrel in skillet. Cover and cook over low heat for 1 hour.

Suckerfish and Whitefish *(Nez Perce Telling)*

Suckerfish and Whitefish were good friends.

One day a child got married and the time came for the two fish to go wedding trading. They took everything to the host's house.

The host made some porridge and set it in front of them. The suckerfish took a half-burned log and used it as a spoon to eat the porridge. The hot, burning "spoon" made his mouth become thick and bulged out. While eating, he said, "It would take five armloads of wood to cook me."

Whitefish drank the porridge with a straw. "I can be cooked with anything that will burn, even a straw."

This is why the suckerfish has thick, turned-out lips, and why the whitefish has a small, pointed mouth. One ate porridge with a burning stick and the other ate it with a straw.

Whitefish will cook with a small amount of fire. To cook a suckerfish, you must use a lot of fire and cook it a long, long time. Even then, it barely cooks.

Fried Whitefish *(Modern)*

2 lbs. dressed whitefish
1 tsp. salt
2 eggs, beaten
½ cup flour
¼ cup cornmeal
¼ cup bread crumbs
Fat for frying

Salt fish and dip in eggs, then coat with mixture of flour, cornmeal and bread crumbs. Fry in hot oil for 4 to 5 minutes on each side.

Grasshoppers and Ants *(Traditional)*

Grasshoppers are edible when hard portions, such as wings and legs, have been removed. Termites, locust and crickets are similarly eaten.

Ants have an acidity which appealed to natives. They were often consumed by mashing them in water sweetened with berries or sap. The eggs and the young of the ants were also eaten.

Diggers Indians, of the Shoshoni Tribe, ate large quantities of insects. They lived in the most barren portion of North America.

Helen's Potatoes and Watercress Soup *(Modern)*

5 medium potatoes
A few handfuls of watercress
1 Tbsp. butter
½ cup milk
4 cups water
Salt and pepper

Chop potatoes very fine. Add with other ingredients to kettle and cook 10 minutes to heat through, but do not boil.

Indian Potato Indian Potatoes grow on open mountain sides and ridges in sandy, gravelly soil throughout Montana to western Colorado, west to Utah and Washington.

Dig up the small tubers in the fall. The tubers need not be peeled and can be eaten raw, boiled or pit roasted.

Jerky Gravy *(Modern)*

4 cups jerky pieces
3 Tbsp. fat
3 Tbsp. unbleached flour
2 cups milk

Pound jerky into a coarse powder with a hammer or heavy stone. Put in heavy skillet with fat. Blend flour into mixture over low heat until flour has thickened. Slowly add milk, stirring constantly until thickened. Serve over biscuits, wild rice or boiled potatoes.

The men are served meals first. The host waits until all his guests have been served and has eaten before partaking of food himself. Guests are urged to eat heartily and they are expected to eat all put before them or invite others to eat what they cannot. A host is offended if any guest refuses to eat anything offered him.

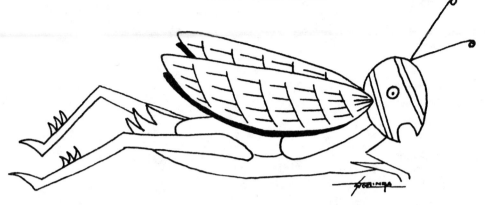

Nettle Soup *(Modern)*

Gather young, stinging nettles in the early spring when they are four to six inches tall. Rinse them, then steam in water left clinging to leaves.

In a kettle, melt some butter. Add a little flour to make a paste. Stir in milk to desired thickness. Rub cooked nettles through a sieve and add to soup. Heat.

Paiute Deer Chops *(Modern)*

6 deer chops
Fat
Unbleached flour
Sat and pepper

Dredge chops in flour, salt and pepper, and fry in fat in heavy skillet. Make gravy from pan drippings, if desired.

Flathead Bitterroot Telling

In the land that is now known as Bitterroot Valley, a great famine came and children went hungry. An old woman, wife of a medicine man, grieved for her starving children.

She went to a stream and bowed low, her face to the earth and her gray hair spread upon it. Bitter tears fell as she chanted the death song.

The sun heard the song of the old woman and called to her guardian spirit, "Comfort her with food and with beauty."

The guardian spirit took the form of a red bird and spoke softly to the old woman, "Your tears have gone to the soil, and a new plant is forming. It will have leaves close to the ground. Its blossoms will first have the rose of my wing feathers and then the white of your hair. Your people will dig the roots and eat it. It will be bitter from your sorrows, but nourishing for your body.

"Your people will see the flowers and will say, 'Here is the silver of our Mother's hair upon the ground by the stream and the rose from the wings of the Spirit Bird. Our Mother's bitter tears have given us food.'"

Pit Roasted Bitterroot *(Traditional)*

Gather bitterroots in late summer as blossoms fade, but before seeds form. Scrub roots with rushes and sand. Rinse well in cold running stream. Dig a pit about one foot in diameter. Build a fire in the pit. Scoop coals from fire and line pit with rushes. Lay roots on top; cover with damp rushes, tree moss and large, green leaves. Cover this with dirt. Make a small fire on top and allow to bake overnight.

"When we were created, we were given our ground to live on and from this time these were our rights. This is all true. We had the fish before the missionaries came, before the white man came. We were put here by the Creator and they were our rights as far as my memory back to my grandfather's. This was the food on which we lived. My mother gathered berries, my father fished and killed game...My strength is from the fish; my blood is from the fish, from the roots and berries. The fish and game are the essence of my life. I was not brought from a foreign country and did not come here. I was put here by the Creator."—Yakima Chief, Weninock, 1915

33

Indian Potato

Pot Roasted Duck (Modern)

2 wild duck
Salt and chili to taste
2 onions, sliced
1 green pepper, cut-up
Bacon
Bacon grease

Season ducks with salt and chili. Stuff cavities with onion and pepper. Wrap bacon around ducks. Heat grease in heavy pot, add ducks, cover, and cook slowly for 2½ hours, adding water once in a while so that it doesn't burn.

Rose Hip Puree (Traditional)

4 cups dried rose hips, seeded
3½ cups water

Cook together rose hips and water, mashing as they cook. Use to flavor soups or serve it with boiled or roasted meat.

The delicate flesh of the Chinook salmon, caught from May to September, was smoked over fires and packed in grass baskets lined with fish skin, for later use. Fish oil, a delicacy to flavor berries and a cosmetic for hair and skin, was contained in gut bags for individual use or trade.

Salmon Baked in Milk (Modern)

4 lbs. salmon
6 slices bacon
4 potatoes, sliced
1 onion, sliced
2 bay leaves
1 cube butter
4 cups milk

Put fish in a baking dish and put two slices of bacon in fish and two slices over. Surround the fish with the potato and onion slices. Add bay leaves. Dot with butter, then cover with milk. Bake at 350-degrees F. for 1 hour.

"I approach the Village,
Ya ha he ha, ya ha ha ha;
And hear the voices of many people,
Ya ha he ha, ya ha ha ha;
The barking of dogs,
Ya ha he ha, ya ha ha ha;
Salmon is plentiful,
Ya ha he ha, ya ha ha ha;
The Berry season is good,
Ya ha he ha, ya ha ha ha."

How Coyote Roasted Salmon
Nez Perce Telling

Coyote was swimming up the Tu-sa (Touchet River in Washington). He saw salmon swimming by and became hungry.

"Come out of the water," he said.

So one of the Chinook salmon swam out to the shore. Coyote grabbed him with a blanket, but the salmon tore up the blanket and swam away. Coyote continued upstream, still hungry.

Soon he saw a meadowlark.

"Tell me," he said to the wise meadowlark, "how can I catch the salmon?"

Meadowlark said, "Tell them to swim out to you and when they near the shore, hit them with a stick."

So Coyote called to the salmon, "Swim to shore!" One did, and Coyote hit him with a club. Then he cut the flesh off and roasted in on a stick. As it roasted, Coyote went to sleep.

Fox, Raccoon and Skunk followed the scent of the roasting salmon and saw Coyote fast asleep. They ate up all the salmon, then cut off a piece of Coyote's rump and placed it on the roasting stick over the fire, and departed.

Coyote soon woke up, saying, "Um, the salmon is cooked and I am hungry." He began feasting on the delicious flesh. An ant crawled up Coyote's leg and when he reached to flick off the ant, he discovered that part of him was gone. He realized that he wast eating his own roasted flesh!

Bitteroot

He looked around and saw Fox, Raccoon and Skunk all laughing at him.

Coyote waited until the three were asleep. He took the yolk of an egg and painted Fox yellow. He took coals from the fire and made circles around Raccoon's eyes and tail. He took ashes and painted a stripe down the back of skunk.

When the three woke and looked at each other, they began laughing. Then they turned and saw Coyote laughing, rolling around on the ground. He had gotten even with them for playing a trick on him.

That is why the river is called Tu-sa, which means to roast something.

Salmon Tail *(Modern)*

1 piece of salmon tail (1½ lbs.)
8 bay leaves

Plunge salmon tail into kettle of boiling water with bay leaves added. Simmer 20 to 30 minutes. Drain and serve.

When a person or family is invited for a meal or a feast, each is expected to bring his own eating utensils.

Sho-Ban Powwow Menudo *(Modern)*

5 lbs. tripe (menudo)
2 calves feet, split and cut into small pieces
4 cloves garlic, minced
2 tsp. salt
1 medium onion, chopped
5 cups cooked hominy
1 tsp. crushed chili pepper
Chopped onion
Fresh chopped tomato
Crushed chilies

Wash menudo and carefully trim all fat. Cut into bite-sized pieces. Put in large pot along with calves feet, garlic and salt. Cook over high heat until all juice is extracted from menudo. Lower heat to medium and cook until menudo is tender, but firm. Add one chopped onion, red pepper and hominy. Cook 10 minutes. Serve in separate bowls with chopped onion, crushed chilies and tomatoes.

Shoshone Teal *(Modern)*

4 teal
1 bunch chopped wild onions
Fat
Wild plums (stoned)
2 Tbsp. juniper berries
1 cup prune juice
2 cups water
Pepper
Watercress

Brown birds and onions in fat 8 to 10 minutes. Remove from pan. Place birds in roasting pan and pour dripping over. Add plums and juniper berries, then pour juice over all. Pour one cup water over birds. Place in 300-degree F. oven and roast, basting frequently with roasting pan juices. Add more water as needed. Sprinkle with pepper. Birds will have cooked in about 2 hours. Cut birds in half and place on a bed of watercress.

Stewed Dried Squawbush *(Modern)*

3 cups squawbush berries
¼ Tbsp. flour
2½ cups boiling water
½ cup honey

Grind berries and mix with flour. Gradually stir this into boiling water and boil 10 minutes. Add honey and serve.

Sunflower Gravy *(Traditional)*

¼ cup fat, cut into tiny pieces
3 Tbsp. finely chopped wild onion
6 Tbsp. finely ground sunflower meal
1 Tbsp. corn flour
2 cups water

Fry fat and onion until translucent. Add sunflower meal and corn flour. Cook one minute, stirring constantly. Slowly pour in water while stirring. Cook until thickened. This was traditionally cooked in a basket with heated stones, or in a buffalo pouch.

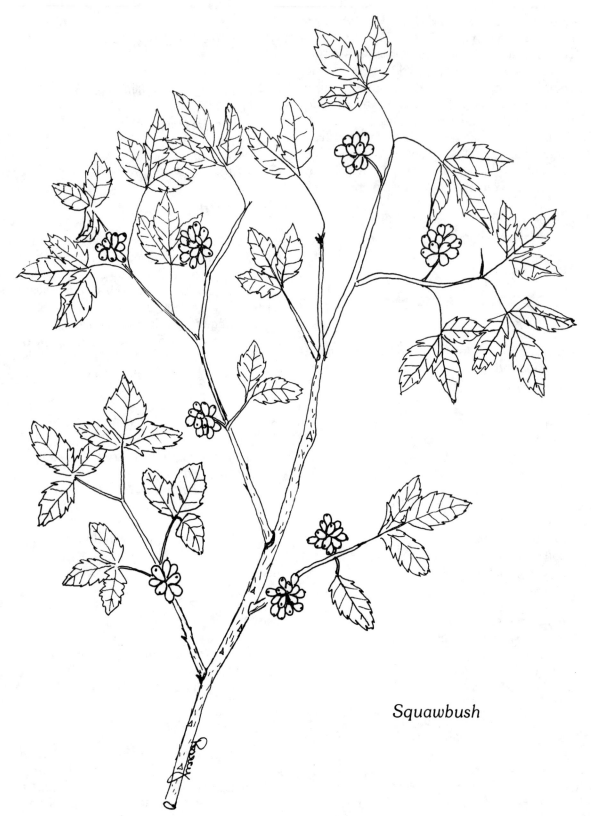

Squawbush

Tumblemustard To gather the seeds, dry over a tanned hide then shake out seed. Clusters of the fruit are picked, placed in a bag and allowed to dry.

Grind seeds and dried fruit (small dried blossoms) into a meal and use in flavoring soups and stews or making gruel.

Venison-Acorn Stew *(Traditional)*

2 lbs. venison, cut up
1 cup finely ground acorn meal

Cover venison with water in pot or basket; add hot rocks to simmer until meat almost falls apart. Remove meat from broth and chop into fine pieces. Return to pot with liquid and stir in acorn meal. Serve hot.

Wild Grape The young tendrils are good eaten raw. The ripe fruit can be squeezed into juice or dried in the sun for future use. The dried fruit can be ground, seeds and all, and used to thicken stews and to flavor bland foods.

Wild Oat *(Traditional)*

Strip the wild oats from the stock and shatter them into a basket. Drop live coals into the basket and shake the mixture so that the long grain hairs are singed off.

Grind the oats into meal, or flatten them by rolling a stone over them. Winnow the chaff out in the breeze. Cook in bread or make a gruel.

The roots and leaves of wild strawberries are steeped into a strong tea and used for ulcers, gums and eye inflammation.

A poultice of the leaves is used to treat choleric stomach, and cleaning the blood and spleen.

Wild Strawberry Sun Preserves
(Modern)

1 lb. wild strawberries
2 cups sugar
1 cup water

Boil together sugar and water until it spins a thread. Remove from heat. Add strawberries and let stand overnight. Pour onto platter or flat clean surface, cover with cloth (do not allow cloth to touch fruit) and set in direct hot sunlight for four days. Stir twice a day.

Bring berries inside during the evening sunset. When preserves finish, pour into covered jar.

Agave

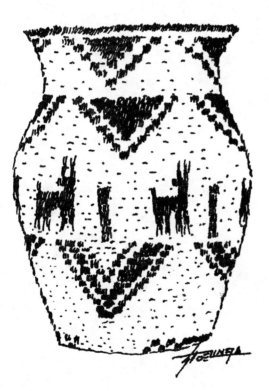

Chapter III

Southwestern Culture Area

The Southwestern Culture Area is comprised of northwestern Mexico, Arizona and New Mexico. The tribes include the Taos, Santa Clara, San Lldefonso, San Domingo, Isleta, Acoma, Zuni, Hopi, Pima Papago, Navajo, Walapai, Havasupai and Apache.

Agriculture provided most of the food for the Pueblos. They grew maize, beans and squash. After the coming of the Spaniards in the 16th century, they began to grow melons, peaches and garden vegetables. The diet was subsidized by antelope, deer and rabbit.

The Pima, Papago and related tribes grew maize, beans and squash, as well. Hunting and gathering wild foods were more important to these tribes than the Pueblo. They hunted deer, antelope and mountain sheep, and gathered such foods as mesquite pods, Arizona walnuts and various cactus, especially the fruit of the Saguaro.

The Navajo, Apache, Walapai and Havasupai depended mainly on hunting and wild plants, although they did eventually develop some agriculture and raised sheep and goat.

41

Prickly Pear

Agave, Roasted (Traditional)

Dig up agave, trim leaves and stems. Make a circular pit, six feet in diameter and two feet deep. Line pit with stones and build a fire upon them, keeping fire hot until rocks are well heated. Brush away ashes and place agave in the pit. Cover with grass and weeds. Top with dirt. Build a fire on top of the dirt and keep tended for two days. Dig up agave.

Pound the baked agave flat and dry in sun. Best soaked in water before eating.

Agave (Mescal or Century Plant) — mashed pulp was used for infections and also as poultice for chest congestion. The leaves were chewed as a tonic. The juice of the root stops bleeding of fresh wounds. The cooked juice of the leaves was used as a remedy for scurvy.

Agave Buds (Traditional)

Gather agave buds just before they open. Place in water in tightly woven basket and drop in heated stones until water is boiling. Eat when buds become tender, or drain cooked buds and fry in hot mutton fat for three to four minutes.

"When Usen (Apache God) created the Apaches, He also created their homes in the West. He gave them grains, fruits and game as they needed to eat. To restore their health when disease attacked them, He taught them where to find these herbs, and how to prepare them for medicine."
— Geronimo

Apache Rabbit (Traditional)

Wash and cut up cottontail rabbit. Cover with water and cook until about done. Remove from liquid, dust with cornmeal and fry in fat until brown.

Take the lung of a newly killed sheep, allow blood to drain from it, then press all clear liquid from the drained lung. Keep the clear liquid in a glass bottle to use on warts. Rub warts frequently with liquid and they will soon disappear.

Backbone Stew (Traditional)

6 ears fresh corn
4 cups water
10 3- to 4-inch pieces mutton backbone
Saltbush

Cut corn from ears and put in pot along with water, mutton and some saltbush. Cook for 1½ hours.

Batter-Fried Squash Blossoms (Modern)

3 dozen squash blossoms, picked just before they open
1 cup goat's milk
1 Tbsp. flour
Dash hot chili pepper
1 tsp. salt
½ cup corn oil

Combine milk, flour and seasoning. Dip blossoms into batter and fry in hot oil until golden brown.

In very lean times, old people would eat only once every three days in order to leave food for the children.

Blood Sausage (Traditional)

5 cups sheep blood
2 cups ground sheep fat
1⅔ cup cornmeal
2 tsp. salt
1½ tsp. crushed red chili pepper
3 cups raw, peeled, grated potatoes
Clean stomach of sheep

43

Desert Hackberry

With hands, mix together blood and fat. Add cornmeal, salt, chili pepper and potatoes and mix well with hands. Put mixture in stomach and tie up with string. Place in pan, cover with water and boil for 1½ hours.

Breaded Nopalitos (Modern)

5 to 6 nopalitos (prickly pear pads)
1 egg
1 cup milk
¼ tsp. salt
¼ tsp. pepper
1½ cups cornmeal
Butter or bacon drippings

Remove spicules and skin from cactus pads. Parboil in water to cover 10 minutes. Drain. Cool. Cut pads into fourths.

Beat together egg, milk, salt and pepper. Dip nopalitos in mixture, then roll in cornmeal. Sauté in butter or bacon drippings until crisp and brown.

Prickly Pear   The split leaves or pads are used to bind wounds. This greatly speeds up the healing process. The roasting split pads are applied and bound on chin and neck to reduce swelling of mumps and rheumatism. Warmed, split pads applied to breasts encourage the flow of milk.

Dried Cactus Tunas (Prickly pear fruits)

To dry, dig a pit two feet deep. Make a fire that will burn down to a good bed of coals and cover coals with a two-inch layer of saltbush twigs. Layer despined cactus fruits on top. Cover with hot rocks. Make another layer of fruit and then more hot rocks until pit is full. Add a final layer of saltbush and cover with dirt. Leave overnight. Uncover, lay baked fruit on flat rocks and dry in sun.

Dried fruits are cooked by boiling or stewing.

Cholla Campfire (Modern)

Bacon drippings
1 rattlesnake or cottontail, cut into serving
*   sized pieces*
1 onion, sliced
½ cup rice
1½ quarts water
2 cups peeled, chopped cholla buds
2 cloves minced garlic
2 Tbsp. cornmeal
Salt and pepper to taste

In Dutch oven over campfire, brown meat and onion in oil. Add remaining ingredients and simmer 1 hour. Add more cornstarch toward the end of cooking time, if a thicker stew is wanted.

Cholla (Jumping Cactus or Staghorn)   A tea made from the roots is used as a remedy for diarrhea. Baked buds, which have been ground, is used for stomach ailments and ulcers.

French Fried Yucca Shoots (Modern)

2 lbs. yucca shoots
1 tsp. baking powder
1 tsp. garlic salt
2 small eggs, slightly beaten
1 cup milk
1 Tbsp. salad oil
Lard for deep frying

Peel yucca shoots and cut into strips. Soak strips in salted water overnight. Drain and rinse.

Mix together baking powder, flour, and garlic salt. Combine eggs, milk and oil; gradually add to flour mixture, beating until smooth.

Dip yucca strips into batter and fry in deep hot lard at 375-degrees F. for 2 to 3 minutes.

Drain on paper towels. Sprinkle with salt and serve at once.

Greenthread Navajo Tea *(Traditional)*

Gather the plant along open plains and slopes. Tie the plants into small bundles and dry them in the shade.

Drop a bundle into boiling water for a few minutes until it becomes yellowish-green in color.

Ground Cherry (Tomatilla)   The berries can be eaten raw, cooked in sauces, or mixed with chili peppers and wild onions for salsa.

If the outer covering is left on the fruit, it will keep for a long period of time.

Ancient Mesa Verde Indians were believed to have cultivated the ground-cherry.

Hackberry Leather *(Modern)*

4 cups hackberry puree
¼ cup honey

Mix puree with honey. Spread thinly on clean, dry board or waxed paper. Suspend cheese cloth over puree to keep insects from fruit. Allow to dry, then peel from surface. Roll up and wrap in plastic wrap or waxed paper. Store in covered containers.

Hopi women pride themselves on their ability to bake piki bread, an art which takes practice and patience. A hopi girl may propose marriage to a boy by leaving a plate of piki on his doorstep. Her mother and an uncle accompany her. If the boy and his family take the bread in, the proposal is accepted. Otherwise, a member of the girl's family returns to remove the plate of bread.

Hopi Piki Bread *(Traditional)*

1 cup green juniper ash
1 cup boiling water
3 cups water
1 cup blue cornmeal
Sunflower oil for greasing stone

Mix ash with boiling water. Strain juniper ash into pot. Stir. Add blue cornmeal. Stir with wooden spoon or stick. Let cool. Spread on hot, greased griddle or stone with palm of hand. Be certain the layer is very thin. Cook for a very short time. Carefully, lift paper-thin layer from griddle by rolling from one end to the other, jelly-roll fashioned.

Indian Flat Bread *(Traditional)*

⅔ cup green juniper ash
1 cup whole grain flour
½ cup cracked grain
Water
Sunflower oil

Burn green juniper (not the branch part) until you get ⅔ cup of ash. Mix with flour and cracked grain. Add water to form stiff dough. Knead briefly. Pinch off pieces of dough the size of walnuts. Flatten each between palms of hands until dough becomes very thin. Fry each flattened piece in oil, on each side, until crisp and lightly browned.

Indian Sun Bread *(Modern)*

2 pkgs. active dry yeast
6 to 6½ cups flour
2 cups water
3 Tbsp. melted fat
1 Tbsp. sugar
½ tsp. salt

Combine yeast with 2¼ cups flour in mixing bowl. Heat water, shortening, sugar and salt. Add to flour mixture. Beat until well mixed. Add remaining flour and knead until smooth and elastic. Place in large, greased bowl. Cover and let rise in warm spot until doubled in bulk.

Corn Planting Time Song *(Hopi)*

In May, corn planting time, a "Korosta Kachina Dance," in which the Kachina wear masks painted with the rainbow, this song is sung. The song is about the butterflies flying over the corn fields and over the beans. One butterfly is running after the other like the hunt, and there are many pairs.

Even as the Hopis paint their faces for a ceremonial dance, so have the butterflies for their flight over the corn blossoms, painted themselves with pollen.

The butterflies must go through many flowers, say the Hopi, to make themselves so pretty.

Korosta Katzina Tawg	*Korosta Kachina Song*
Sikta Vocimu	Yellow Butterflies,
Humisi Manatu	Over the Blossoming Virgin Corn,
Talasi Yammu	With Pollen-Painted Faces
Pitzangwa Timakiang	Chase One Another
Tuve-Nanguyimani	In Brilliant Throng
Shakwa Volimu	Blue Butterflies,
Mozhisi Manatu	Over the Blooming Virgin Beans,
Talasi Yammu	With Pollen Painted Faces
Pitzangwa Timakiang	Chase one another in
Tuve-Nanguyimani.	Brilliant Steams.
Humisi Manatu	Over the Blooming Corn,
Amunawita	Over the Virgin Corn,
Tatangayata Tokiyuywintani	Wild Bees Hum.
Mozhisi Manatu	Over the Blooming Virgin Beans,
Amunawita	Over the Virgin Corn
Tokiyuyuwintani	Wild Bees Hum.
Umuh Uti	Over the Field of Growing Corn,
Amunawit	All Day Shall Hang the Thunder Cloud;
Tawanawita	
Umuu Uti	Over Your Field of Growing Corn
Amunawit Yoi-Hoyoyotimani	All Day Shall Come the Rushing Rain.
Tawanawita.	

Punch down; divide into thirds and shape each into a ball. Let rest for 10 minutes. Roll each ball into a 9-inch circle. Fold each circle almost in half so that top edge is ½-inch from bottom edge.

Place in greased baking sheets. Make 6 gashes in dough, cutting two-thirds of the way inward towards folded edges. Spread strips of dough apart so that they don't touch. Let rise in warm place until doubled.

Bake at 350-degrees F. for 45 to 50 minutes.

Midge's Navajo Reservation Macaroni and Cheese *(Modern)*

Government issued:
    Macaroni
    Cheese
    Powdered milk
    White flour
    Salt

Cook up 3 cups macaroni. In pan, mix up 4 cups milk from the powder and heat. Add about 2½ cups of cheese and stir it up until cheese melts. Mix some white flour with a little water to make paste. Thicken cheese mixture with paste and add drained cooked macaroni. Salt. Pour in a dish and bake in oven until it firms up.

Ocotillo Ice *(Modern)*

    8 cups ocotillo blossoms
    1 pint water
    1½ cups sugar
    Juice of 2 lemons

Bring water and sugar to boiling over medium heat without stirring. Cover and turn off heat. Allow to stand covered for 5 minutes. Pour over ocotillo blossoms and allow to stand until syrup has cooled. Discard blossoms. Add lemon juice to syrup and mix well. Freeze in freezer trays. Serve as you would sherbet.

Ocotillo (Slimwood/Coach Whip) — a tea from the roots relieves fatigue and painful swelling.

Nopalitos are the young pads of the prickly pear cactus and are harvested when one to three inches in diameter. The stickers are scraped from the pads after they have been boiled for 30 minutes. Traditionally, the cleaned pads were cut into strips or squares, boiled until tender, then eaten unseasoned.

Today, the pads are served in numerous ways, many reflecting Mexican origins.

Jalapeno-Nopalitos Corn Pudding *(Modern)*

    2 cups diced cooked nopalitos, well drained
    1½ cups creamed corn
    1 cup cornmeal
    1 cup melted butter
    ¾ cup evaporated milk
    2 medium onions, chopped
    2 eggs, beaten
    ½ tsp. baking soda
    2 cups grated sharp Cheddar cheese
    3 fresh jalapeno peppers, minced

Combine first 8 ingredients and mix well. Turn half into a 9-inch square baking pan. Cover evenly with half cheese, then peppers, then remaining cheese. Bake in preheated 350-degree F. oven for 1 hour. Cool 15 minutes before cutting into squares. Serves 9.

Juniper Tea *(Traditional)*

    30 tender young juniper shoots
    2½ quarts water

Combine shoots and water in kettle. Boil gently for 15 minutes. Turn heat off and let steep for 10 minutes. Strain and serve.

Kneeldown Bread *(Traditional)*

Scrape kernels from fresh corn, then grind to a mush on a metate. Add a little salt, if desired. With hands, form into cakes 3-inches long and 2-inches wide and 1-inch thick in center. Steep corn shucks in hot water until pliable. Fold one shuck over each cake with narrow ends turned under.

Dig a pit 2-ft. square by 9-inches deep. Make a fire in pit. When well heated, rake fire out. Place a layer of prepared corn cakes in pit with succeeding layers over it until all are used. Put wet corn husks over top and cover all with dirt and hot ashes. Build a small fire over all. Bake slowly overnight.

Lambs Quarter Gruel

Gather the small, dark seeds of the Lambs Quarters in late summer or early autumn. Pound seeds into a course meal, add to 2 parts water and cook until gruel reaches desired thickness. Add more pounded seeds if a thicker cereal is desired.

Navajo Clabbored Goat's Milk
(Traditional)

> *2 white horse nettle berries*
> *1 quart goat's milk*

Crumble berries into goat's milk and boil for 7 to 10 minutes. Drain off liquid and eat at once.

Navajo Fry Bread (Modern)

> *4 cups unbleached flour*
> *1 cup dry milk solids*
> *1½ Tbsp. double acting baking powder*
> *½ tsp. salt*
> *¼ cup lard cut into ½-inch pieces*
> *1 cup ice water*
> *Lard or oil for deep fat frying*

Sift together dry ingredients. With pastry cutter, or fingers, cut ¼ cup lard into flour until like cornmeal. Quickly add water and stir briskly with wooden spoon until dough forms. Cover and let rest in warm place for two hours. Divide into 6 pieces. Flatten each into an 8-inch circle. Poke hole in center with finger.

Melt lard in 10-inch skillet until hot, but not smoking (melted fat should be at least 1-inch deep). Fry each circle 2 minutes on each side. Drain on paper towels.

Hunter's Stew (Traditional)

> *Deer meat, cubed*
> *Wild garlic*
> *Chopped prickly pear leaves*
> *Lard*
> *Chopped chiles*
> *Any available tubers*

Dredge meat in flour and fry in lard until brown. Remove to large pot. Sauté wild garlic and nopalitos in same lard until tender-crisp. Add remaining ingredients and pour into pot with meat. Add some water and simmer until meat and tubers are tender.

Navajo Juniper Corn Bread (Modern)

> *½ cup juniper ashes*
> *½ cup boiling water*
> *½ cup flour*
> *2½ cups cornmeal*
> *½ tsp. salt*
> *1 cup boiling water*
> *Heavy duty aluminum foil*

Burn green juniper until you get ½ cup ashes. Mix in ½ cup boiling water.

In pot, bring 1 cups water and ½ tsp. salt to boiling. Add ash mixture and stir well. Mix flour with cornmeal and stir into ash mixture. Cool. Knead until dough is soft and firm. Shape into a loaf and wrap in foil. Place in bed of coals and bake 1 hour, turning frequently.

Navajo Mutton Loaf (Modern)

> *3 cups finely diced cooked mutton*
> *1½ cups canned tomatoes, diced*
> *1 cup fresh bread, crumbled*
> *1 small onion, chopped*
> *1 tsp. salt*
> *½ tsp. crushed juniper berries*
> *1 egg*

Combine all ingredients in bowl and mix with hands. Form into loaf and put in loaf pan. Bake at 400-degrees F. for 45 minutes.

Navaho Hunting Song

When the traditional Navajo hunter prepares for the hunt, he first prays to the God of Game, then sings a holy song, followed by the hunting song. If he misses a word, or makes an error, he will not have a successful hunt. But if the song is sung without error, the game will come to him.

The hunter positions himself along the game trail and sits motionless as he chants the hunting song. The animals are curious and drawn to the rhythm of the song.

In this song, the hunter becomes a beautiful blackbird loved by the deer. This bird alights on the deer and sometimes tries to make its nest between the horns. The song tells of the coming of the deer—how he makes a trail from the top of the Black Mountains down through the fair meadows, how he comes through the dew-drops and the pollen of the flowers, and then how, startled at the sight of the hunter, he stamps and turns to run. But the man kills him for he is blessed in hunting.

The Navajos say that the male deer always starts with the left foreleg, the female with the right.

Navajo Lamb Spareribs (Modern)

4 lbs. spareribs
¼ cup melted butter
¼ cup mesquite honey
¼ cup lemon juice
½ tsp. slightly crushed cumin seed
2 tsp. grated onion
1 tsp. dried oregano
2 sprigs wild garlic or 2 garlic cloves, minced
Flour
Salt and pepper

Heat together butter, honey, lemon juice, seasonings, onion and garlic.

Rub mixture of flour, salt and pepper into ribs. Grill ribs 5 minutes over hot coals. Baste with sauce and turn frequently for 20 or more minutes.

Navajo Taco (Modern)

6 rounds Navajo fry bread
1½ lb. ground lamb
1 Tbsp. lard
½ lb. sharp cheddar cheese, grated
1 head iceburg lettuce, shredded
3 ripe medium tomatoes
1 can diced green chilies
1 cup chopped green onion
Salsa (optional)

Brown lamb in lard. Divide among the six fry breads. Sprinkle with cheese, lettuce tomatoes, chilies and green onions. Serve with salsa, if desired.

Papago Pipian (Traditional)

A sauce for meat or vegetables
3 Tbsp. lard
1 cup crumbled corn bread
1 tsp. chili powder
2 cloves garlic, minced
1 cup dried squash seeds, ground
1½ Tbsp. unbleached flour
1 Tbsp. honey
3 cups water

Melt lard in skillet. Add bread, chili powder, garlic and seeds. Stir and cook until ingredients are toasted. Stir in flour and honey. Slowly add water and cook, simmering, until thickened.

Papago Squash (Modern)

2 lbs. summer squash, cut into small pieces
½ lb. grated Cheddar cheese
1 cup cooked, diced nopalitos

Cook squash in salted water until tender. Drain and put layer of squash in greased casserole, sprinkle with one half of the diced nopalitos and one half of the grated cheese. Put remaining squash in casserole and add remaining nopalitos and cheese. Bake at 400-degrees F. for 20 minutes.

Navajo wild Potatoes *Wild potatoes thrive from Texas to Arizona and north to southern Colorado and Utah.*

Boil potatoes until tender. Drain and mash between grinding stones. Dissolve a small handful of salt clay in water and add to the potatoes as they are being mashed. Mold into small loaves. Good served with mutton broth or goat's milk.

51

Pueblo Corn-Grinding Song

Plateau Pinon Soup *(Traditional)*

1 wild turkey carcass
Wild carrots
Wild onions
Wild garlic
Sheppard's purse seeds
Any wild greens
½ cup ground pinon nuts
Water

Place carcass in large pot, cover with water and add vegetables. Simmer until broth looks strong. Strain. Add wild greens, pinons and meat from carcass.

Pueblo Adobe Oven Bread *(Modern)*

1 pkg. yeast
½ cup warm water
5½ cups unbleached flour
2 Tbsp. lard
1 tsp. sugar
2 tsp. raw sugar
1½ cups hot water

Dissolve yeast in warm water. Add lard, salt and sugar to hot water in large bowl. Add 1 cup flour and beat well. Add yeast mixture and mix. Add 3 to 3½ cups flour and mix well.

Turn onto floured board and knead, adding more flour until elastic. Place dough in oiled bowl, invert and cover with towel. Let rise until doubled in bulk. Divide in half. Form into round loaves. Let rise, covered, until doubled. Bake at 350-degrees F. for 1 hour.

The practice of piping soothing music into factories is by no means an invention of the modern age. Writing of the Pueblos, Castaneda depicted this domestic scene in 1540:

"They keep the separate houses where they prepare the food for eating and where they grind the meal, very clean. This is a separate room or closet, where they have a trough with three stones fixed in stiff clay. Three women go in here, each one having a stone, with which one of them breaks the corn, the next grinds it, and the third grinds it again. They take off their shoes, do up their hair, shake their clothes, and cover their heads before

Pueblo quail

they enter the door. A man sits at the door playing on a fife while they grind, moving the stones to the music and singing together."

Pueblo Corn Cakes *(Modern)*

2 large handfuls of cornmeal
4 eggs, beaten
1 Tbsp. baking powder
Lard or oil

Mix together cornmeal, eggs, baking powder and enough water to form a stiff batter.

Mold into cakes ½-inch thick and 2½ to 3-inches in diameter. Fry in hot fat or oil until golden brown.

Pueblo Greens and Beans *(Modern)*

Small pieces of chopped mutton fat
1 lb. tumbleweed or other greens
¼ cup chopped onion
2 cloves garlic, minced
½ cup water
½ tsp. salt
3 cups cooked pinto beans

Cook mutton fat until crisp. Add greens, onion, garlic, water and salt. Cook until greens are wilted and add beans. Heat through.

53

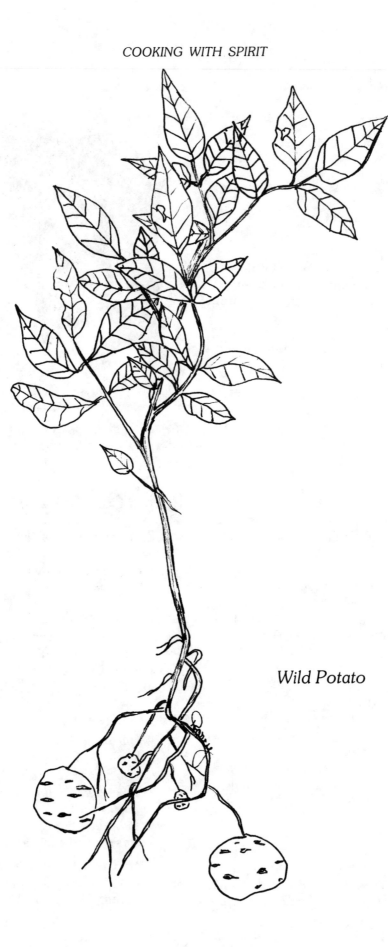

Wild Potato

Pueblo Succotash *(Traditional)*

1 cup chopped onion
2 chopped tomatoes
½ tsp. chili powder
1½ cups dried corn, cooked
1½ cups cooked lima beans
½ cup sunflower seeds

Combine ingredients and heat through.

Every year traditional Apache families hold a pumpkin ceremony to ensure a bountiful crop. While the pumpkin vines were still young, a small boy was sent out to gather juniper berries. When he returned, he was blind-folded and sent to the pumpkin patch. He then threw the juniper berries in all directions, asking for an equal number of pumpkins.

Pumpkin with Corn *(Traditional)*

Cut green corn from cob and mash well. Peel and cut pumpkin into cubes. Add equal amounts of pumpkin and corn to kettle. Add enough water to cover and cook until pumpkin becomes tender. Add a handful of sunflower seeds. Cook and stir until very soft.

Purslane Large quantities of purslane was dried by spreading the young stems out in the hot sun on roofs. It was later to be cooked in water as a potherb.
The plants are also gathered while they are fruiting, placed on flat rocks or canvas and left to dry in the sun. The seeds are then minnowed and ground into meal.
Purslane is also good raw.

Rattlesnake *(Modern preparation for cooking)*

Cut off the head and bury it. Slit skin to two inches below wound and peel back. Tie cord or heavy string around area where skin has been peeled back. Hang snake by string, leaving both hands free to remove skin. With sharp knife, loosen skin from flesh as you work skin down along the body. Once skin had been removed, slit the belly open and remove intestines. Rinse snake in salted water. Cut into serving sized pieces.

May be coated with flour and fried as you would chicken, or thrown into the stew or soup kettle.

Papago and neighboring tribes feasted on the June ripened fruits of the Saguaro. Fruits were knocked from the towering cactus by using saguaro ribs. The fruit hulls would usually split open upon hitting the ground. The pulp was then scooped out of the split hulls and placed into water tight baskets. The black seeds were separated from the pulp to be ground and used for bread. The sweet pulp was used in many ways, such as syrup, dried pulp and jams.

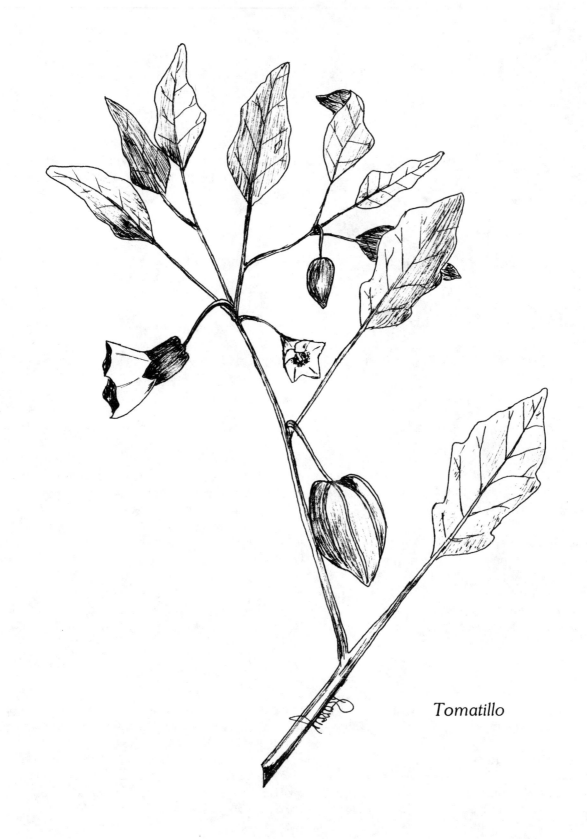

Tomatillo

Saguaro Porridge *(Modern)*

1 quart saguaro pulp
1 quart water
1½ cups white cornmeal
1 cup sugar
¼ tsp. salt

Combine pulp and water in top of double boiler and place over simmering water. Heat until pulp mixture begins to steam. Stir cornmeal into pulp mixture and cook over simmering water for 20 minutes. Add sugar and salt. Stir well. Remove from heat and beat with electric mixer on low speed until cool Serve with cream.

Saguaro Seed Bread *(Traditional)*

1 handful ground saguaro seeds
½ handful ground sunflower seed
Large handful blue cornmeal
Saguaro pulp mixed with water

Combine seeds and cornmeal. Add enough saguaro-water mixture to form a medium stiff dough. Knead well on smooth stone.

Dig a pit 6-inches deep and 18-inches in diameter. Build fire in pit and let burn for four to five hours. Rake ashes from pit and line bottom and sides with wet corn husks, overlapping. Place dough on husks. Cover with another layer of wet husks. Add layer of dirt and hot coals. Build small fire on top and keep fire burning low for four to five hours. Uncover pit and serve bread.

Southwest Adobe Bread Pudding
(Modern)

4 cups stale Pueblo Adobe Oven Bread
½ cup sugar
¼ tsp. salt
½ tsp. ground cinnamon
¼ tsp. ground ginger
2 eggs, beaten
1 quart milk
½ cup dried currants
2 Tbsp. melted butter

Combine sugar and spices in large bowl. Beat in eggs. Slowly add milk. Mix in bread, currants and butter.

Pour into greased 9-inch square pan and bake at 350 degrees F. for 1 hour, or until straw comes out clean.

Sunflower Seeds *the seeds were gathered, parched and often eaten whole since the thin hulls are not as coarse as the cultivated sunflower.*

Sunflower oil was made by grinding the entire seeds, then boiling the mass until oil rose to the surface. This was skimmed off and used as cooking oil.

Hopi Indians still use sunflower oil for greasing their hot flat rock for Piki Bread.

"When Chief Lololomai prays he goes to the edge of the cliff and turns his face to the rising sun, and scatters the sacred cornmeal. Then he prays for all the people. He asks that we may have rain and corn and melons, and that our fields may bring us plenty. But these are not the only things he prays for. He prays that all people may have health and long life and be happy and good in their hearts. And Hopis are not the only people he prays for. He prays for everybody in the whole world— everybody. And not people alone; Lololomai prays for all the animals. And not animals alone; Lololomai prays for all the plants. He prays for everything that has life. That is how Lololomai prays."—Lololomai, Hopi Chief.

The Hopi ate a salty clay with wild foods such as Tomatilla berries. This particular clay has the properties of counteracting the acid in such foods which would otherwise make the food inedible.

Tomatilla *(also see Ground Cherry) Tomatilla grows along dry plains and hills. The berries are eaten fresh or dried for winter use. They can be cooked into a sauce, spread out on rocks and allowed to dry. This can be stored for later use and recooked into a sauce or soup. The raw fruit was frequently mixed with equal parts of salt clay before being eaten.*

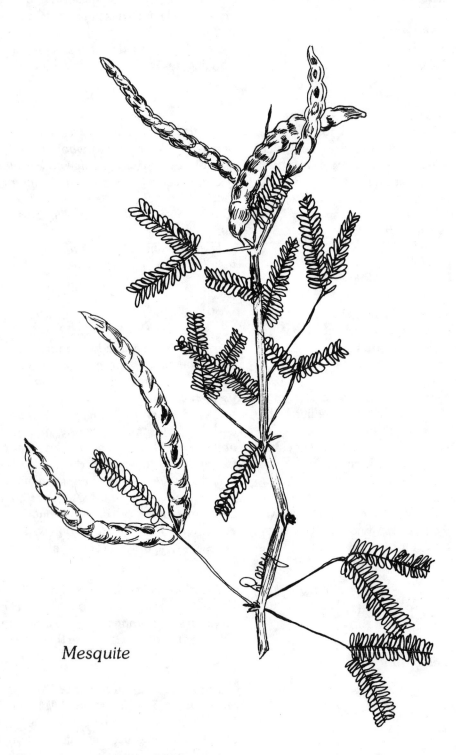

Mesquite

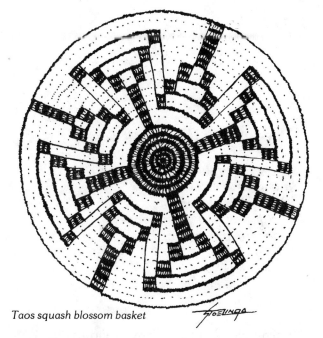

Taos squash blossom basket

Wild Fowl Walnut Dressing *(Modern)*

½ loaf stale bread
Some salt
Some sage and few juniper berries, crushed
3 handfuls of wild walnuts
Some fat
1 onion, chopped

Crumble bread and toss with salt, sage, juniper and walnuts.

Cook onion in fat until softened. Mix with bread. Add a little water to moisten some. Stuff birds. Wrap birds in aluminum foil and bake over hot coals or bake in 350-degree F. oven for 45 to 60 minutes, depending on size of bird.

Black Walnut Hulls   *Juice used for worming and ridding the body of lice and parasites. A dark brown hair dye was made from steeping the hulls in hot water. Hulls rubbed on the flesh relieves some of the aches of rheumatism. Place hulls in bath to relieve leg cramps.*

Women of the Yuman tribes traditionally prepared two meals per day. The first was prepared before dawn. The evening meal's preparation began at mid-day, after native foods were gathered from the desert. Much time was spent pounding the hard mesquite beans or grinding wild seeds.

Most of the foods were baked in hot ashes instead of being boiled. This helped conserve precious water.

Yuman Mesquite Gruel *(Traditional)*

3 cups water
⅔ cup finely ground and sifted mesquite pods
⅓ cup finely ground sunflower seed
½ cup ground desert hackberries

Boil together for 25 to 30 minutes, or until thickened.

Mesquite   *black gum was used as hair dye; when diluted with water, as a wash for sore eyes and wounds; and as an ointment for chapped, cracked lips or sunburn.*

Boiled inner bark was used as an emetic or cathartic.

Leaves were made into a tea for headaches, stomach ailments, and rinse for sore gums.

Yucca   *Various yucca bear fruit. Yucca baccata is fleshy. Gather fruits and split open, scrape out seeds and pulp and eat fresh. The fruits can also be roasted or boiled. When boiling, remove seeds and skin, and cook down to a paste. This is formed into cakes and dried to be later used in gruel, dumplings or bread.*

Other groups of yucca have dryer fruits. Bake these fruits in hot ashes. They can then be sliced and dried for future use. If fruits are mature, remove the seeds; if not, they may be eaten, seeds and all.

"Sickness comes with you (white man) and hundreds of us die. Where is our strength?...In the old times we were strong. We used to hunt and fish. We raised our little crop of corn and melons and ate the mesquite beans. Now all is changed. We eat the white man's food and it makes us soft."—Chiparopai, old Yuman woman

59

Yuma Reservation Fried Meat *(Modern)*

Government issued:
- **Canned meat**
- **Powdered eggs**
- **White flour**
- **Vegetable shortening**

Open canned meat and slide out of can. Slice meat into 1½-inch slabs. Mix powdered eggs with water. Dip meat slices in eggs and roll in flour. Fry in hot melted shortening until crispy.

The sun rules plants with parts resembling it in shape and color, such as camomile and sunflowers. The sun also rules medicinal plants affecting the heart, such as eyebright and walnuts.

The moon rules plants with parts similar in shape and color, such as gourds, melons, pumpkin and squash, and some plants with white or yellow flowers such as sweet flag and water lillies. The moon also rules plants with high water content and soft, juicy leaves such as cabbage, lettuce and leafy vegetables; and plants which live in or near water — seaweed, willow, watercress.

Zuni Sunflower Pudding *(Traditional)*

- **1 cup fresh green corn kernels**
- **1 cup coarse sunflower meal**
- **1 cup finely chopped summer squash**
- **1 ¾ cups water**
- **½ tsp. salt**

Grind together corn kernels and meal. Add to saucepan along with squash, water and salt. Cover with tight fitting lid and simmer 1 hour. Remove lid and continue to cook until mixture is thick and gelatinous.

Zuni Vegetable Relish *(Modern)*

- **2 cups finely shredded cabbage**
- **½ cup grated carrot**
- **½ cup chopped onion**
- **½ cup chopped green pepper**
- **1 medium onion, diced**
- **1 Tbsp. sugar**
- **½ tsp. salt**
- **½ tsp. chili powder**
- **¼ cup vinegar**

Combine all ingredients, cover and refrigerate overnight.

Chapter IV

The Plains Culture Area

The Plains Culture Area includes the Black-feet, Crow, Arapaho, Cheyenne, Comanche, Pawnee, Omaha, Iowa, Sioux, Mandan, Hi-datsa and Kiowa. The area extends from Texas, north into Canada and from the Missis-sippi River to the Rocky Mountains.

The nomadic tribes of the plains hunted buffalo, elk, deer and antelope. Both farming and nomadic hunting tribes ate berries, choke cherries, wild turnips, wild rice and acorns.

Maize, beans, squash, pumpkin and sun-flowers were the principal crops of the farming tribes.

The Blackfeet never ate turtles, frogs or lizards, for they believed these were creatures of evil. Dog, though eaten by Crees, Gros Ventres, Sioux and other surrounding tribes, were never eaten by the Blackfeet

Blackfoot Beavertail Stew (Traditional)

1 beaver tail
Wild onions
Wild tubers
Wild carrots

Skin and cut beaver tail into 1-inch cubes. Boil for a couple of hours with the vegetables.

Beavers eating birch taste better than those that eat aspen.

Wild Onion   Used for flavoring foods or eaten raw. Used as a blood purifier for all ailments. Lowers blood pressure, regulates action of liver and gall bladder, stimulates activity of digestive organs and relieves problems of digestion.

The Blackfeet make buckets, cups, basins and dishes from the lining of buffalo's pouch. This was torn off in large pieces and was stretched over a flattened willow or cherry wood hoop and the bottom was sewn to the pouch, which came down over it, doubled on the exterior. Needle holes were sealed with tree pitch. The hoop at the upper edge was also sewn to the pouch, and a rawhide lace was passed under it, forming a carrying handle.

Breadroot   Thrives in prairies and plains on open, rocky ground. Dig roots in July or August when the leaves begin to turn brown. Peel and boil until tender, or pit roast unpeeled. May also be baked in the hot coals of a campfire. Unused cooked roots can be dried in the sun and stored for future use. The dried root is often ground into meal and used for thickening soup, making gruel and baking in bread.

Buffalo Pouch Stew (Traditional)

Thoroughly clean buffalo pouch. Punch four small holes through four corners of pouch and fasten pouch to a tripod of four green poles by threading thongs through holes and securing each to one of the four poles.

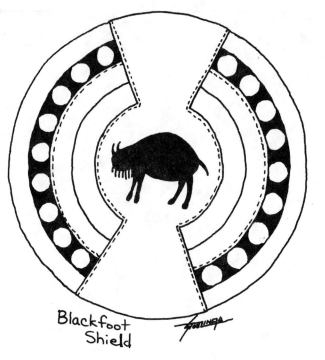

Blackfoot Shield

Build a fire and heat ten fist-sized rocks until very hot.

Meanwhile, fill suspended pouch half full of water. Add small pieces of buffalo meat, wild turnips and any other available wild edible roots.

When rocks are very hot, pick up one with two forked sticks and place in pouch. Add another stone. Liquid in kettle will boil. Add another stone when needed, removing cooled ones. Cook until meat and vegetables are tender (approximately 45 minutes). First stew inside pouch is eaten, then the pouch itself is consumed.

"I can remember when the bison were so many that they could not be counted, but more and more Wasichus (white man) came to kill them until there were only heaps of bones and scattered where they used to be. The Wasichus did not kill them to eat, they killed them for the metal that makes them crazy and they took only the hides to sell. Sometimes they did not even take the hides, only the tongues, and I have heard that fire-boats come down the Missouri River loaded with dried buffalo tongues. You can see that the men who did this were crazy. Sometimes they did not even take the tongues; they just killed and killed because they liked to do that. When we hunted bison, we killed only what we needed."   —Black Elk, Sioux Chief

Buffalo Steaks (Modern)

Buffalo steaks, 1" thick
Pepper corns
Salt
3 or 4 garlic cloves

Pound together seasonings and rub over steaks. Grill on a broiling rack 3" from coals until desired doneness.

Bush Morning Glory   *These plants grow in sandy soils and dunes. Select bush morning glory roots which are three or more inches in diameter. Slice into pieces ½-inch thick and peel off tough outer rind. The white core is excellent when eaten raw.*

Often the unpeeled root was pit roasted. uneaten portions were formed into cakes and dried.

Coal Roasted Buffalo (Traditional)

Have meat at room temperature. Rub roast with wild garlic. Place directly on hot coals and cook 15 to 20 minutes per pound for rare roast; 20 to 25 minutes per pound for medium roast. Cook on coals, turning occasionally until all sides have a charred coating.

"A long time ago this land belonged to our fathers, but when I go up to the river I see camps of soldiers on its banks. These soldiers cut down my timber, they kill my buffalo, and when I see that, my heart feels like bursting. I feel sorry...

"Has the white man become a child that he should recklessly kill and not eat? When the red men slay game, they do so that they may live and not starve." — Satanta, Chief of the Kiowas

Comanche Prairie Chicken with Sweet Potatoes (Modern)

2 prairie chickens
Flour, salt and pepper
4 to 6 sweet potatoes or yams, peeled and sliced
Fat
1 cup sorgum syrup
½ cup chopped pecans

Dredge birds in flour, salt and pepper and brown on all sides in fat. Place birds in baking dish with sliced yams around them. Pour sorgum over and sprinkle with pecans. Cover and bake at 350-degrees F. for an hour or until tender.

Cow Parsnip   *Dig up the roots and peel them. Boil them in water until they become soft, then mash them up. With a little salt, they are good.*

Crow Chokecherry Pudding (Traditional)

Coarsely mash ripe chokecherries and cover with water. Boil 15 minutes, thicken with arrowroot and sweeten with sugar.

The American Indians have many uses for chokecherries. They use the inner bark to ease pain during labor. Juice of the chokecherries was allowed to ferment for a year, then taken as a cure for dysentery.

It is always a mark of distinction to be served dog. Before the Indians had horse, the dog was their best animal friend. So when a man sacrificed his dog friend for his visitors, he was really demonstrating the high esteem he held for his guests.

Dog Stew (Traditional)

Dig a 1½-ft. wide by 2-ft. deep pit. Line with stones and wet green prairie grasses. Form hide of dog, hair side down, over stones and grass lining. Lay dog meat on hide. Add wild turnips, wild onions and wild garlic. Fold hide over meat, forming pouch. Cover with numerous layers of wet green prairie grass and small stones. Build fire on top and burn until there are plenty of hot coals and stones are hot. Cover with earth and allow to steam five to six hours before uncovering pit.

Cheyenne Buffalo Dance Song

The Elk

Old Man was very hungry. He had been a long time without food. He saw a band of elk on the ridge and cried, "Oh, my brothers, I am lonesome because I have no one to follow me."

"Go on, Old Man," said the elk, "we will follow you." Old Man led them about a long time, and when it was dark he came to a steep bank. He went around to one side where there was a slope and stood under the steep bluff.

"That was a nice jump, you will laugh!" he called out to the elk. So the elk jumped off. One pregnant cow was afraid to jump, and the Old Man let her go so that there would be plenty of elk someday.

All the elk that jumped died in the fall. The Old Man built a fire and cooked some ribs, then he skinned all the elk, cut up the meat to dry and hung the tongues on a pole.

The next day he went off and did not return until dark, when he had grown hungry again.

"I will roast some ribs and a tongue," he said. But when he got to the place, the meat was gone. The wolves had eaten it. And the mice had eaten the meat out of the tongues, leaving only the skin. So Old Man starved again.

Elk Stew *(Modern)*

3 Tbsp. bacon fat
3 lbs. elk, cubed
5 potatoes, peeled and cubed
6 carrots, sliced
1½ cup chopped onion
½ cup sliced celery
½ lb. sliced mushrooms
2 cloves garlic
Salt and pepper
1 cup water

Brown meat in bacon fat in Dutch oven. Add rest of the ingredients, cover and cook 2½ hours.

Gussie's Wild Plum Preserves *(Modern)*

With a sharp penknife, cut a long slit in each plum. Spread in dishes and set in sun till the seed comes out readily. Then boil till thoroughly done in a thick syrup made of as many pounds of sugar as there are pounds of plums.

Wild Plum   *August is the Moon of Ripe Red Plums. A tea made from the root is used to expel worms. The fruit and bark are used as a mild astringent and laxative. The inner bark is used in gargle for sores of the mouth and throat.*

The people use woods from various trees for their cooking and serving utensils because of their flavoring and healing qualities which are passed into the foods they prepared.

The same is thought true of the shells, skins and feathers that are made into clothing, shelter, ceremonial apparel and implements.

Hidatsa Buffalo Blood Broth
(Traditional)

Take 1½ to 2 gallons unclotted blood and pour into large kettle. Add 1 cup water and 1 piece of buffalo marrow fat twice the size of an egg, 2 handfuls of dried, cooked winter squash and bring to a boil.

Prepare stirring paddle of chokecherry sappling, fraying bark at one end to render a cherry flavor.

Prepare another stick by stripping bark from small twig. This is used to dip into broth. If blood clings to stick, continue boiling; if stick comes out clean and white, broth is ready to eat.

Hildy's Buffaloberry Jelly *(Modern)*

Wash and crush berries. Boil slowly for 10 minutes, stirring. Put in jelly bag and drain off juice. To each cup juice add 1 cup sugar. Bring to boil and cook until it jells. Pour into hot jelly jars.

Indian Lettuce or Miner's Lettuce   *This succulent plant grows along moist banks and slopes in partial shade from the Rocky Mountains east to Northeastern Arizona, Eastern Utah and the Black Hills of South Dakota. It is eaten raw and found in early spring through early summer.*

Chokecherry

Stone bowls were sometimes fashioned by the Plains People. A rock would be selected, then light blows from a heavier stone would begin a hollow. The hollow was made deeper by pounding and grinding. When deep enough, the bowl would be filled with water and set in the cook fire.

Jerusalem Artichoke Dig tubers in the fall. Eat raw or roast in coals. Roasted tubers may be flattened between palms and dried for future use.

The Jerusalem artichoke is easily recognized. It is a tall, coarse sunflower with broad, rough leaves and rough, hairy stems. Upper leaves alternate; lower leaves are often opposite.

Josephine's Squashberry Jelly
(Modern)

> **4 cups ripe squashberry juice**
> **1 pkg. pectin**
> **Juice of one lemon**
> **6 cups sugar**
> **2 cinnamon sticks**
> **6 cloves**

Crush eight cups of well ripened squashberries. Add lemon juice and ½ cup water. Heat to boiling and simmer 10 minutes. Add sugar and boil 1 minutes longer. Stir and skim. Pour into jelly glasses and seal with parraffin.

Lena's Water Crackers *(Wind River Reservation)*

> **1 lb. commodity flour**
> **1 tsp. of salt and the same of soda**
> **1 big tablespoonful of vegetable shortening or lard**

Make up with some powdered milk to form a dough and beat it up, roll thin and bake quickly.

Blackfeet often boiled meat in a green hide. A hole was dug in the ground and lined with skin, flesh side up, being supported along the edges of the hole by pegs. Meat and water were placed in the skin. Red-hot stones were dropped in the water until it boiled and the meat lost its red color.

Mariposa Lily The whole plant provides food. The stem, flower and leaves are good raw. Seeds can be ground as food and the green seed pods eaten raw.

The bulbs, located five to six inches underground can be washed and outer husk rubbed off and eaten raw. They can be roasted, fried, steamed or boiled.

In a local town cafe, two cowpokes were drinking coffee and complaining about how the government was letting in too many aliens, who took American jobs, and how the country was going to the dogs. About that time, two Indians, wrapped in blankets, came in to get out of the cold. Upon seeing them, one cowpoke remarked to the other, "See what I mean, Sam? More darn foreigners!"

Pit Barbecued Venison *(Modern)*

Dig a 2-ft. wide by 2½-ft. deep pit. Line with numerous layers of wild grape or maple leaves. Lay haunch of venison on leaves. Surround it with sweet potatoes, carrots, onions, unhusked sweet corn (silk removed) and cloves of garlic. Cover with another layer of leaves. Cover with stones which have been heated in a campfire. Add a few layers of hot embers or charcoal. Cover all with wet burlap, add more embers and cover well with dirt so that no steam escapes. Uncover pit after four or five hours.

The name Assiniboine comes from a Chippewa Indian term that signifies "one who cooks by the use of stones." Hence, the Assiniboines are often called Stoney Indians or Stoneys.

All parts of the buffalo, elk, deer and antelope were often eaten with the exception of lungs, gall and a couple of other organs. The paunch, or stomach, was eaten raw, as was the liver. The unborn calf of a freshly killed animal was a great delicacy. The small intestines of the buffalo were turned inside out and stuffed with long, thin strips of meat, then roasted until the juices flowed. The ends were then tied and the "sausage" was boiled until cooked.

Buffalo Berries

Pit Roasted Antelope *(Traditional)*

Dig a pit 2-ft. wide and 2-ft. deep. Line the pit with stones. Add more stones to lined pit and build a sagebrush or willow wood fire in and around the pit until there is a good quantity of embers. Remove embers and stones (leaving stones lining the pit in place). Line pit with fresh antelope hide, hair side down. Place chunks of antelope meat on hide and fold the flesh side over to cover meat. Place embers and hot stones on top of hide and cover entire hole with dirt. Open pit five or six hours later.

Mimbres antelope

Kiowa Lullaby
Okum Daagya

A-Go-Go
T'oph'o Goan-kontono
T'anba ok'un-balita.

Hush thee, child
Mother bringest an antelope,
And the tidbit shall be thine.

If a mother's milk was insufficient, remedies known to be effective in increasing the flow were given to her, and other nursing mothers acted in her place until she was cured of the deficiency. Artificial baby foods are not a modern invention. Primative Indian women knew how to prepare formulas that were nourishing, using broth made from buffalo or deer meat, mashed corn and other ingredients.

Pawnee Prairie Chicken *(Modern)*

1 cleaned prairie chicken
Flour, salt and pepper
Onions and celery
Fat

Dredge bird in flour, salt and pepper and brown in fat on all sides. Stuff onions and celery in cavity and around bird in baking dish. Cover and bake in 325-degree F. oven for 1 hour, or until tender. Baste occasionally with drippings.

Corn Mother *(Pawnee)*

Corn told man that she is mother. If a grain of corn be split, within it will be found a juice like mother's milk. So the corn is mother, because she nourishes.

Hither the Mother-Corn—
Greet we the Mother-Corn—
Thanks to the Mother-Corn—
Now she cometh
Hither the Mother-Corn!
He Yo!

Indian Corn (Maize) Corn silk is used in diuretic preparations for urinary problems as cystitis. It is also good as a dieting food.

69

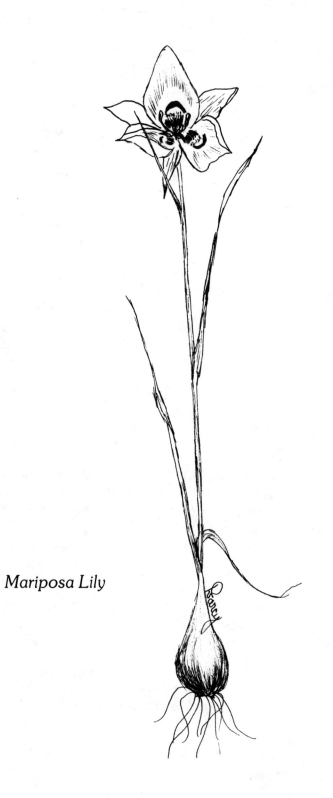

Mariposa Lily

Plains Corn Bread *(Traditional)*

1 pint cornmeal
Cold water to make a stiff dough

Work well with hands, pat out in long, narrow pones. Bake quickly over hot coals or in hot cast iron skillet.

Father de Smet, the first religious man to reach many parts of the American West described how some Assininbion women prepared a feast at which he was a guest:
"If a bit of dried meat or any other provision is in need of being cleansed, the dainty cook filled her mouth with water and spurts it upon the object.

"A certain dish is prepared in a most singular manner and they are entitled to a patent for the happy faculty of invention. The women commence by rubbing their hands with grease, and collecting in them the blood of the animal which they boil with water. Finally they fill the kettle with fat and hashed meat. But—hashed with the teeth! Often half a dozen old women are occupied in this mincing operation for hours, mouthful after mouthful is masticated, and thus passes from the mouth into the cauldron, to compose the choice ragout of the Rocky Mountains.

"Add to this, by way of an exquisite dessert, pulverized ants, grasshoppers and locusts that have been dried in the sun…"

Plains Muledeer Stew *(Traditional)*

4 lbs. muledeer, cut-up
Wild grain flour
Fat
Some chopped wild onions
Some chopped wild carrots
Some chopped Prairie Turnips or cattail
  root chips
Juniper or buffalo berries

Sprinkle meat with grain flour and brown meat in fat in kettle. Add onions and other vegetables along with some water to consistancy desired. Simmer over low fire until tender.

Wanagi Wacipi Olowan
Spirit Dance Song of the Sioux

He, he, wanna wawate,
He, he, wanna wawate,
Wasna Watinkte,
Wasna Watinkte!

Hey, hey, joyous feast we now,
Hey, hey, joyous feast we now,
Eating Pemmican,
Eating Pemmican!

Plains Pemmican *(Traditional)*

Dry long, thin strips of buffalo meat. Pound meat to a coarse powder. Cut raw fat into walnut-sized pieces and melt over slow fire. Pour fat over pounded meat and mix in some dried serviceberries. Mix it well and pack in parfletches.

It normally takes the meat of two buffalo cows to make a one-hundred pound bag of pemmican.

Popped Wild Rice *(Traditional)*

Plains Indians would paddle their canoes among wild rice plants, bend the seed laden stalks over the craft and beat the grains out onto the floor or their canoes.

Place a small amount of freshly gathered wild rice in a small woven basket. Immerse basket in a container of deep, hot bear or buffalo fat until kernels pop. Remove basket immediately, letting fat drain from basket. Eat at once.

Wild Rice

Blackfoot Telling

One time Old Man was walking and came to a place where many squirrels were playing in hot ashes. While some of them lay in the ashes, the others would cover them with more ashes. When the buried squirrels became so hot that they could not stand the heat any longer, they would call out to the others who would take them out at once. After Old Man had watched them for awhile, he asked that they allow him to play with them.

When the squirrels consented, he asked, "May I be baked first?"

"Oh, no," they replied, "we are afraid that you do not know how to play, and that you would be burned. We will be baked first to show you how."

Old Man again asked, and again they refused. At last, Old Man agreed with them, on the condition that they would let him cover all of them at one time.

"There are so many of you," he said, "that it will save some time to bury all of you at once."

The squirrels consented. So he covered all of them with hot ashes except one that was about to become a mother. She pleaded so pitifully not to be put in the ashes that Old Man said, "Run away, so that there may be other squirrels."

When all the others were well covered with ashes, some of them became too warm, and called to Old Man to take them out. Instead, he heaped on more ashes and roasted them to death.

Then Old Man took some red willows and made a scaffold on which he placed the roasted squirrels. They made the willows greasy, and that is why the red willow is greasy, even to this day.

And today, squirreling around still goes on and those who squirrel still get roasted.

Roasted Squirrel *(Traditional)*

Clean and skin squirrels. Fill body cavity with any wild edible plants or berries in season. Wrap in many layers of leaves or grass which have been soaked in a stream. Bury wrapped squirrels in hot ashes and lay hot coals on top. Let squirrels roast for 2 hours, replacing coals as needed. Dig roasted squirrels from ashes, unwrap and eat.

Serviceberry *Gather the purplish-red fruit in late summer to early fall. Can be eaten raw or pounded into a pulp and spread out on a flat rock to dry. Often the berries were dried whole and added to dried, powdered meat along with melted fat and marrow to make pemmican.*

Berry picking was generally the job of the young, unmarried girls and old women. Picking aprons were worn by some, while others placed a small hide beneath the bush and dropped the harvest onto it. The supply could then be transferred to skin bags. The women usually brought a dog and travois to transport the harvest.

Men were not exempt from gathering. When an abundance was discovered, a husband and wife might pick together so that the greatest possible amount could be preserved before spoilage occurred.

The Sioux woman so thoroughly surveyed the potentials of native plant life that literally no source of food was overlooked. Indeed, it was a common practice for the old woman to probe new campsites in search of a mouse's cache of dried beans.

Shepherd's Purse *The ripened fruits are gathered, dried and the seeds beaten out. The seeds are ground into a meal and mixed with a variety of other meals and flours for breads. The pods and seeds are used to flavor soup and stews.*

Young leaves are good raw. The fresh or dried roots are used as a flavoring, having a ginger-like flavor.

Starving Elk's Telling

Once upon a time, the people were camped in a circle, and in the center, they held a game. But the people were hungry; they had nothing to eat.

Now there were two medicine men, holy men, men of mystery, who had dressed themselves in great beauty to go to the game. The first holy man wore a buffalo robe, the second wore one also. The two medicine men looked at each other. They were dressed exactly alike, their faces painted alike, and their feathers arranged the same way.

Said the first holy man, "Are you against me that

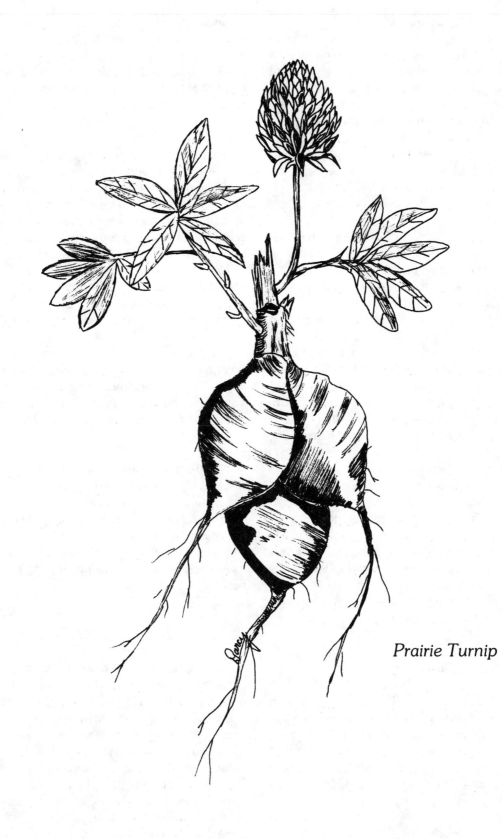

Prairie Turnip

you imitate my dress? Are you mocking me?"

And the second answered, "It seems that you are mocking me. Where did you learn to dress like this?"

Then the first said, "In a dream I went to the clear spring that is near the camp, and there in the spring, I learned this dress."

And the second said, "I, too, went to the spring in a dream, and there I learned this dress."

Then they argued, and at last they said, "Go we together to the spring by open day and let us prove which has the better right to wear this dress." So they set out and all the people followed.

When they came to the spring, each one said defiantly to the other, "Dare you go in?"

So they stepped in together and sank to the very bottom. There they saw an old woman who lived in the spring, and she asked of them, "What do you want here?"

Now they both were hungry, and they answered, "Our people have nothing to eat."

So the woman gave each a bowl of food to take back with him. In the one bowl, she put corn, and in the other, pemmican.

So the two holy men went back to their people and gave them the food, and they all ate of it, the whole tribe, even the little children. Yet, however much they ate, the two bowls never emptied.

Thus, there came to the Cheyenne the food on which they live—meat and corn.

Stuffed Sugar Pumpkin (Modern)

> 1 3-4 lb. sugar pumpkin
> 1 tsp. salt
> 1/2 tsp. dry mustard
> 1 onion, chopped
> 1 lb. ground venison
> 3 eggs, beaten
> 1 cup cooked rice
> 1/2 cup water

Cut lid out of pumpkin and remove seeds. Prick inside cavity with fork. Rub inside with salt and mustard.

Cook onion and venison in skillet with a little fat until browned. Add eggs and rice. Stuff pumpkin with mixture.

Bake in shallow pan with 1/2 cup water for 1 1/2 hours or until tender.

In times of plenty, great quantities of meat were prepared for use when fresh meat could not be obtained. The thick parts of the animal were sliced into large, thin sheets and hung to dry, either outside in the sun or hung on lines in the upper part of the lodge.

The back fat of buffalo was also dried and smeared on the dried meat to be eaten.

Sioux Jerky (Traditional)

In making jerky, follow the natural contours and muscle layers. Do not cut cross-grain.

Cut into very thin slices. Hang on poles or drying racks, high enough so that dogs cannot reach them.

Do not fret about flies; the meat will be too thin and flies cannot lay eggs in it. Make certain pieces do not touch one another. At night, pile on clean surface and cover, then rehang come morning. When meat is hard and dry, it is ready to eat.

Pound to a powder to make pemmican. Or cook in water until soft.

Steamed Silverweed Roots (Traditional)

Dig up a quantity of roots. Steam in a pit lined with hot stones by placing roots and covering with layers of wet grass. Layer dirt on top. Uncover pit after three hours.

"Hey-a-a-hey! Hey-a-a-hey! Hey-a-a-hey! Grandfather, Great Spirit, once more behold me on earth and learn to hear my feeble voice. You lived first, and you are older than all need, older than all prayer. All things belong to you—the two-leggeds, the four-leggeds, the wings of the air and all green things that live, you have set the powers of the four quarters to cross each other. The good road—the road of difficulties, you have made to cross and where they cross, the place is holy. Day in and day out, forever, you are the life of things..." —Portion of Black Elk's Prayer, 1931

Wild Prairie Turnips During late June and early July, dig prairie turnips. Peel turnips, braid together root tails and hang up to dry. After drying, they are soaked in water, and then boiled.

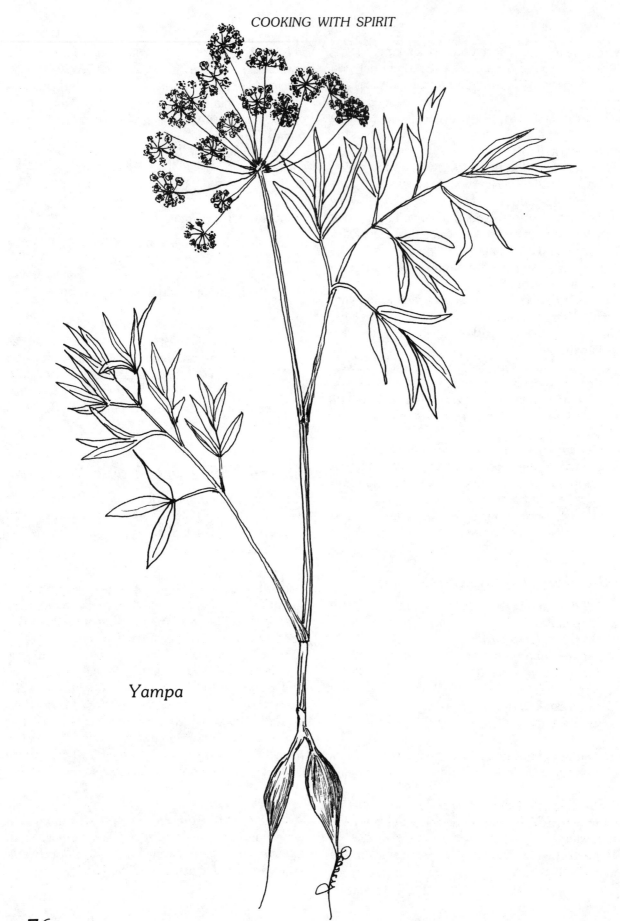

Yampa

Sioux painted parfleche

Sioux Prairie Turnip Pudding *(Traditional)* *(Traditional)*

Harvest and dry prairie turnips in the sun. Pound the dried roots into a flour and mix with water and buffalo berries. Cook in a buffalo paunch pot with hot stones.

Washtunk' Kala *(Traditional Sioux Winter Soup)* *Soup)*

Break jerky into small pieces and put in suspended buffalo pouch. Add some dried prairie turnips, dried squash, dried corn and dried berries. Add water to pouch.

Heat stones and drop in pouch, removing those which cool. Soon soup will be boiling. Boil until jerky is tender.

Waterfowl Eggs *(Traditional)*

In the spring, many people of the plains had great feasts of waterfowl eggs. When a large quantity had been gathered, a hole was dug in the ground about 3 feet deep. The bottom of the hole was packed tightly to retain water. A little water was poured in. At short intervals above the water, platforms of reeds and sticks were built. Eggs were laid on the platforms. A smaller hole was dug at one side of the big hole, slanting to the water. The big hole was covered with grass, twigs and mud.

Stones were heated red hot in a campfire. These stones were rolled down the little hole so that they would hit the water, heating it. The eggs were steamed cooked this way.

Yampa *(Traditional)*

Gather the yampa roots in late summer or early autumn and place them in large baskets. Submerge the basket in a running stream, then tread on the yampa with bare feet. This removes the thin, brown skin. The roots can now be eaten raw or baked, pit roasted, boiled and then dried.

Creamed Yampa *(Modern)*

Boil and peel 6 cups of yampa roots. Set aside. Melt 2 Tbsp. of butter or bacon grease in pot, add salt and pepper to taste. Stir in 2 Tbsp. flour and cook until well blended. Slowly stir in 1 cup milk. Add yampa roots and heat through. Serve at once.

Many of the plants are healers and grow in families or tribes. They can be sun plants or moon plants, their sap or "blood" moving with the rising and setting of the sun (male) or waxing and waning of the moon (female). There is a chief (sun) or mother (moon) plant that is the guardian of the family and it is to them an offering is made (usually tobacco or corn pollen) in exchange and recognition of their healing powers. These are considered "warrior" plants because of their ability to grow and endure by nature's means. Their medicines are strong as they come from the survival of the fittest.

When any leaf or stem, flower or root is taken, consideration is given as to where the sap's power is most prevalent. In a sun plant where one would use just the flower, it was picked around noon when the sun was at or around its apex. Should the leaves or stem be needed, there were taken in the morning or afternoon when the sun was rising or setting. The roots are taken at night and usually at full moon. The best seasonal time is also of importance. With moon plants the process is, of course, reversed.

When medicine is sought for healing, one must bear in mind that plants taken with consideration and reverence, that medicine will have far superior curing power because of the care and knowledge that went into its harvest One cannot harm one living being and then expect to use it to cure another. For example, taking a plant without consideration created an imbalance. Therefore, the purpose of healing is thwarted or defeated, as a balance of health is what is sought in the first place.

This is also carried over to the appropriating of food from the plant, fish, bird and animal beings.

American Lotus

Chapter V

Southeastern Culture Area

The Southeastern Culture Area includes the tribes of the southeastern portion of the United States including the Natchez, Taensa, Choctaw, Chickasaw, Cree, Cherokee, Seminole, Yuchi, Catawba, Tuscarora, Powhatan and Miccosukee.

The area extends south of the Ohio River and Pennsylvania and east to the Mississippi River.

Almost all of the southeastern tribes were farmers who grew maize, beans, pumpkins, sunflowers and squash. Those who lived in southern Florida and in the southwest of the region did not farm, but lived off the land hunting bison in the interior and fishing on the coast. Deer and bear were also hunted, as were birds and small game.

American Lotus—Found in quiet waters from Texas to Florida, Minnesota to Massachusetts. Most abundant west of the Appalachians.

The young, unfurled leaves are gathered and cooked like spinach, the large tubers are baked, the immature seeds are eaten raw, the ripe seeds are roasted, ground and minnowed, making a good flour to be mixed with grain flours for breads or cooked into a gruel.

G. RAILSBACK

Poke

COOKING WITH SPIRIT

Corn was a gift from the Native Americans to world agriculture. Before Columbus, the food was unknown in the Old World.

To the American Indians, corn is the sustainer of life and provides a major symbol in the rituals of numerous tribes.

Catawba Corn (Modern)

Pull husks back from corn and save. Discard silk. Blend salt, pepper, freshly minced parsley, freshly minced garlic and softened butter. Spread mixture over each ear of corn and twist shut. Place on hot coals and bake, turning occasionally, for 12 minutes.

Wild Yam   Root is used as an antispasmodic, diuretic, expectorant, soothing of the nerve and pain in the urinary tract.

Catawba Potato Cakes (Modern)

3 large sweet potatoes, cooked and mashed
2 eggs
1 tsp. salt
¼ tsp. nutmeg
Lard

Mix together mashed sweet potatoes, eggs, salt and nutmeg.

Heat lard on griddle. Drop potato mixture from large spoon onto fat and brown on both sides. Serve hot with butter.

An Ancient Cherokee Telling

In the beginning times of earth life, rocks, plants, creepy-crawlers, fish, animals and man lived together in equality and mutual helpfulness in a beautiful balance of nature. The needs of all were met in a world of plenty.

Soon the harmony was disrupted as man became more aggressive in his relationship with earth's environment—caring less and less for the rights and privileges of his creature relatives. Overcome with greed and his increasing desire for power, man multiplied rapidly. An imbalance of nature's creativity was caused by his claiming more than his share of territory and food, thus dwindling the chances of his fellow creatures' survival.

The relatives became alarmed and held council. An alliance against their brother, man, was formed, and many diseases were devised to hinder his encroachment over earth. The bond between man and his relatives was broken.

And so, sickness and procurement of food became difficult for man and many methods were used to appease the spirits of creatures he killed for nourishment.

Even so, many plants and mineral relatives remained loyal to man, and knowing of his many afflictions, offered themselves to help remedy them—if only they would be discovered and applied.

For nourishment and health, man needed to consider his relationship with all that lived, offering equal and giving exchange. Thus, through the ages, the delicate balance of securing food and medicine in a reverent manner, making certain that his relatives would survive and flourish, continuously develops among man.

Cherokee Bean Ball (Modern)

4 cups cooked and mashed brown beans
½ cup bean cooking liquid
4 cups cornmeal
½ cup unbleached flour
1 tsp. baking soda

Combine all ingredients and mix well. Roll dough into egg-sized balls and drop in boiling water. Simmer 30 minutes.

Golden seal is used by the Cherokees as a remedy for stomach disorders, sore mouths, inflamed eyes and infections. Their remedies became adopted by early pioneers and settlers.

Cherokee Bread Pudding (Modern)

2½ cups stale bread cubes
2½ cups scalded milk
1 cup butter
½ cup sorgum
Pinch of salt
2 eggs, slightly beaten
½ tsp. maple flavoring
¼ cup dried currants

Pour scalded milk over bread. Let stand five minutes. Heat together sorgum, butter and salt. Gradually pour over mixture. Cool. Gradually pour mixture over beaten eggs. Stir in flavoring and currants. Pour into a greased casserole, place in pan of hot water and bake at 350 degrees F. for 50 to 60 minutes or until firm.

Choctaw Corn Pudding (Modern)

Take one dozen large ears of corn. Cut off the top of the grain and scrape with a knife to get the heart of the grain without the husk. Season with cream, a spoonful of butter and salt and pepper to taste. Bake in a dish.

Choctaw File' Kombo (Modern)

1 chicken, cut-up
¼ tsp. salt
¼ tsp. cayenne pepper
3 Tbsp. lard
2 ham hocks
3 Tbsp. flour
1 onion, chopped
1 tomato, chopped
1½ quarts boiling water
1 bay leaf
8 live crayfish
2 Tbsp. butter
½ cup sliced okra
1 Tbsp. file' powder

Sprinkle chicken with salt and cayenne. Brown in lard. Remove chicken. Add flour to drippings and stir until brown. Add onion and cook until golden. Add tomato and cook a few minutes. Gradually add water, stirring. Add ham hocks and chicken along with bay leaf. Simmer slowly until meat is nearly tender. Bring to boiling, add crayfish and okra; cover and simmer briskly for 10 minutes. Remove from heat. Slowly stir in file. Serve over a bed of steamed, wild rice.

File' Powder (Traditional)

Gather young sassafras leaves in early spring. Spread in single layer between two screens or hang in bunches to dry in sun. When leaves are crisp and crumbly, grind to a powder, then put through a sieve. Store in covered containers until needed.

Conch (Modern)

4 conch
2 cloves garlic, crushed
Juice of 1 lemon
¼ cup oil
1 Tbsp. chopped parsley

Place conches, shell and all, in kettle and cover with boiling water. Cover tightly and cook slowly over low flame for 1 hour or until half the conch protrudes from shell. Remove conch and place in cold water. Pull meat out of shells and cut off hard outer skin. Cut meat into ½-inch slices and cover with a mixture made from remaining ingredients. Serve cold.

When fruits, vegetables and herbs come into their natural seasons, this is the time that our bodies are most open to their life-giving and healing spirits.

Chocktaw Poke Greens (Modern)

Pick tender young shoots, boil in water to cover; pour off water and rinse. Add water to cover and simmer until tender. Drain well.
Toss with bacon drippings and serve at once.

Pokeweed Greens can be used as a laxative; dried root for relieving pain, reducing inflammation, treating arthritis and rheumatism, skin parasites and diseases. Juice from the fruit was used in treating cancers, hemorrhoids and tremors.

Coal Roasted Alligator Tail (Traditional)

Take tail of alligator and lay it in a hot pit and cover well with coals. Let this cook for some time (3 to 6 hours, depending on size of tail). Split tail and eat.

Cornmeal Pancakes *(Modern)*

½ cup sifted flour
½ tsp. salt
1 tsp. baking soda
2 cups yellow cornmeal
2 eggs beaten
2½ cups buttermilk

Sift together flour, salt and soda. Stir in cornmeal. Add eggs and buttermilk and beat until lumps are gone.

Pour ¼ cup batter for each cake onto lightly greased, hot griddle. Bake until golden on both sides.

Creek Batter Fried Frog Legs *(Modern)*

1 egg, beaten
½ cup cornmeal
½ tsp. salt
¼ tsp. pepper
2 lbs. frog legs
½ cup lard

Mix together egg, cornmeal, salt and pepper. Dip frog legs in batter and pan fry in melted lard heated in heavy skillet. Fry 20 to 25 minutes.

Elsie's Barbequed Squirrel *(Modern)*

Put some slices of bacon in an oven pan. Lay the squirrels on them and lay two slices of bacon on top. Put them in the oven and let them cook until done. Lay them on a dish and set near the fire. Take out the bacon and sprinkle one spoonful of flour in the gravy and let it brown. Then pour in one teacup of water, a spoonful of butter and some catsup. Pour it over the squirrel.

Everglade Alligator Stew *(Modern)*

2 lbs. alligator meat, cut up
½ cup cooking oil
1 onion, cut-up
1 green pepper, cut up
4 or 5 tomatoes, cut-up

1 hot chili pepper, cut-up
1 cup chopped celery
Salt to taste

Brown meat in oil; add the rest of the ingredients. Cover pot and cook for 45 minutes.

Fried Catfish *(Modern)*

1½ cups cornmeal
2½ cups flour
½ cup chopped parsley
Salt and cayenne pepper
2 lbs. catfish fillets
Oil

Combine cornmeal, flour, parsley and seasonings. Dip fillets in mixture and deep fry at 375 degrees F. until golden brown.

Fried Frog Legs *(Modern)*

6 bullfrog legs
Salt and pepper
1 egg
2 cups cracker crumbs
Cooking oil

Skin legs and wash in cold water. Dry well. Season with salt and pepper. Beat egg, dip legs into egg, then into crumbs. Deep fry at 390 degrees F. for 5 minutes.

83

Golden Club

Golden Club *Thrives in swamp water and ponds. Flowers are followed by beanlike seeds which are harvested and cooked. The rootstocks are dug, thinly sliced and dried, then ground up to make a flour. The flour is most often cooked into a gruel by boiling with water for 45 minutes or longer.*

Hush Puppies *(Modern)*

> *1 cup cornmeal*
> *1 cup flour*
> *½ tsp. salt*
> *1 tsp. baking powder*
> *1 onion, grated*
> *½ cup chopped green onion tops*
> *¾ cup milk*
> *1 egg*
> *Oil for deep frying*

Mix all ingredients, except oil, until blended. Drop by spoonfuls into hot oil and cook until golden brown.

Indian Bread *(Modern)*

Beat two eggs very lightly, mix alternately with them one pint sour milk and one pint fine cornmeal. Melt a spoonful of butter and add to mixture. Dissolve one teaspoonful of soda in a little milk and add to other ingredients. Beat hard and bake in pan in hot oven.

Jack-in-the-Pulpit *Corms of the Jack-in-the-Pulpit are a good source of starch. Roast the corms, then grind into flour. This flour needs to be mixed with grain flours when used to make breads. It can be used as is for flavoring fish stews and soups.*

Leather Britches *(Modern)*

> *2 lbs. green beans, ends snapped off*
> *3 quarts water*
> *½ lb. diced salt pork*
> *¼ cup pepper*

String beans on heavy thread and hang to dry for several weeks or longer.

When ready to cook, soak 1 hour in water. Add salt pork and pepper. Simmer very slowly, stirring occasionally, for 3 hours. Add more water, if necessary. Good with corn bread.

Maypop is often called passion fruit. The blossoms of this native fruit are used to treat nervous conditions such as insomnia, restlessness and headache.

Maypop Jelly *(Modern)*

Gather the large, yellow, egg-sized berries from late July to early October. Scoop out pulp from berries and simmer in kettle for 10 minutes. Strain juice through several thicknesses of cheesecloth. Measure 4½ cups juice and add to 1 pkg. pectin. Boil hard for 1 minute, then add five cups of sugar and boil hard 1 minute longer, skimming and stirring. Pour into jelly glasses and seal with paraffin.

Miccosukee Black-eyed Pea Patties
(Modern powwow food)

Cook black-eyed peas, drain and mash well. Mix with enough flour to hold together. Form into patties and fry in vegetable shortening in a skillet until warmed through.

Miccsukee Fried Plantains *(Modern)*

Peel plantains, slice and fry in small amount of vegetable shortening, stirring and mashing as they cook.

Pawpaw *After the first frost of autumn, the pawpaw fruit falls from the tree. It is usually still unripe. Gather the fruit and set them aside until they yield under gentle pressure. Eat the fruit fresh. When you've had your fill, pulp the remainder and spread out on big leaves. Set in sun to dry. Peel dried fruit off leaf and roll it up. Store in covered basket or container for future use.*

Jack-in-the-Pulpit

Persimmon Collect the fruit in fall or winter. When the fruit is very soft it is ready to eat. Persimmons grow on small forest trees. The fruit ripens after the leaves have fallen, but do not attain their full sweetness until after frost. The pulp can be spread on leaves and dried.

Powhatan Squirrel *(Modern)*

¼ cup flour
3 Tbsp. oil
2½ quarts water
4 squirrels, cut up
1 onion, chopped
Salt and pepper

Cook flour in oil until flour browns; add water and when water simmers, add rest of ingredients. Cook in covered kettle for 1½ hours.

Watergrass — All grass seeds are edible, but the watergrass has unusually large seeds and are therefore an excellent flour source. Pick the grass and lay seed heads on a hide or canvas. When the plant has dried, shake the seeds out and minnow them. Heat a large, flat stone in the fire, then spread the seeds on the stone to parch. Grind the parched seeds into flour.

Purslane Bread *(Traditional)*

Gather the minute black seeds of the purslane. Sieve, then mix half and half with wheat flour.

Take 1 pint of this flour mixture and mix with some salt, some cane sugar and one cup water and a cup of good yeast. Set this to rise and when risen, work in about 2 pints of flour. Work it smooth and set it to rise. When risen, add a small piece of fat and work it well again. Let it stand one hour, then bake it slow on hot coals.

Robins, Orlolans and Small Birds *(Traditional)*

Carefully skin and clean small birds. Rub them with fat and salt. Skewer them onto a green branch and roast over an open fire.

Saw Palmetto Cut the spikelike terminal bud at the top of the stem, peel off outer layers. The firm-textured, tender palm heart is eaten raw, fried, boiled, roasted or baked.

Seminole Alligator Steak *(Modern)*

Cut sections of alligator tail into steaks; squeeze a good amount of lime juice over steaks. Mix some salt with some cayenne pepper and sprinkle this on the steak. Turn steaks occasionally so that both sides are well coated with juice. Grill until done.

Seminole Turtle Soup *(Modern)*

Kill sea turtle at daylight in the summer, the night in winter, and hang it up to bleed. Scald it well and scrape outer skin off the shell. Open it carefully, so as not to break the gall. Break both shells into pieces and put in pot. Lay fins, eggs and delicate parts by. Put the rest in the pot with the shells and a good quantity of water. Add onion and some spices.

About an hour before dinner, thicken with flour and butter. Roll delicate parts and eggs in some flour and fry in butter. Add to soup and cook thirty more minutes. (Meat and shells should simmer for 4 to 6 hours.)

To Cook Turtles *(Land variety)*

Drop four turtles into boiling water and boil one hour, then take them out and remove the skin from the legs and feet and replace them in fresh boiling water where they should continue to boil 1½ hours and then take out to cool

When cold, clean them thoroughly, removing the round liver which contains the gall. Cut them into small bits and place them in a stew pan. Add ingredients on hand to make it good, and stew about 20 minutes.

Maypop

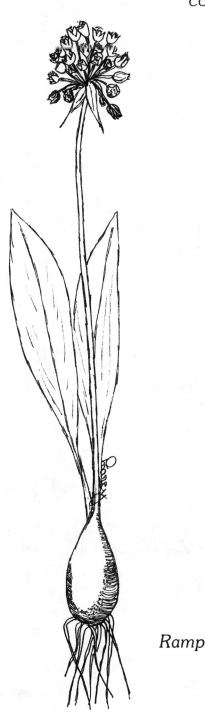

Ramp

Ramp *Several broad, smooth, green, onion-scented leaves appear in early spring. Gather at this time, taking leaves and the bulb to which they are attached. These are sliced and added to stews and soups, or cooked alone. Chop extras and dry them for later use. Look for ramp in moist, rich soils of the deciduous forests.*

Sofkee *(Traditional Creek recipe)*

Pound dried corn into coarse meal, fan with feather to remove husks. Put 2 quarts meal into a large pot of hot water. Place over fire and boil. Fill a perforated vessel or basket with clean wood ashes. Pour water on ashes to form lye. Allow lye to percolate through ashes into meal and water, which will gradually turn yellow. Keep water on mixture for several hours. When mixture becomes very thick, remove from fire and allow to cool. Add pounded hickory nuts and a scoop of bone marrow.

Southern Butternut Pickles *(Modern)*

Gather butternuts while still green and soft, but having obtained their full size. Pour boiling water over unhusked nuts, drain, cool and rub outer fuzz off husks. Put nuts in crock of strong brine, cover tightly and let stand eight days, changing brine every other day.

After eight days, drain and rinse. With needle, prick each butternut several times. Layer nuts in glass jar, sprinkling a mixture of grated gingerroot, nutmeg and cloves between each. Sprinkle a spoonful or two of sugar over all. Pour boiling cider over nuts to cover, seal jars and allow to stand at least two weeks to season.

Wild Duck with Turnips *(Modern)*

1 Tbsp. oil
1 Tbsp. flour
1 onion, chopped
1 cup celery, chopped
1 duck, cut-up
2 turnips, peeled and cut-up
Salt and pepper

Brown flour in oil. Add onion and celery and cook a little while. Put in duck and turnips and brown. Add water to barely cover duck. Cover pot and cook slowly for 1½ hours.

White Pine

Chapter VI

The Northeastern-Machenzie Culture Area

The Northeastern-Machenzie Culture Area lies north of the Ohio River and south to the Arctic, and extends west in Canada to the coastal mountain ranges, which separate it from the Northwest Coast Culture Area. Included in this area are the six nations of the Iroquois—Mohawk, Cayuga, Onenda, Seneca, Onandaga and Tuscaroier. Also included are the Delaware, Huron, Winnebago, Sauk, Fox, Menomini, Ojibwa, Cree, Chipewayan, Beaver, Slave, Kaska, Kutchin and Adirondacks.

The northern-most people hunted caribou, deer, rabbit, bear, moose and game birds. Fish was also an important food, but was usually dried for later use rather than eaten fresh.

Farming tribes grew maize, pumpkin and squash. Two special foods harvested from the wilds were maple syrup and wild rice.

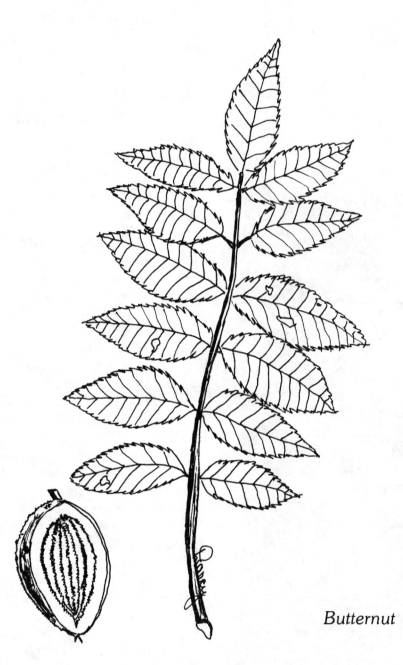

Butternut

Acorn Cakes (Traditional)

Hull acorns and pound into a coarse meal. Place meal in tightly woven basket and place basket in a creek, anchored with stones so that water flows freely through basket but does not flow over top. Leave basket in stream until the following day.

Mix acorn meal with equal amount of ground cornmeal. Add enough water to make a stiff dough. Form into cakes and bake on flat, hot stone.

The Adirondacks were known among Eastern Indian tribes as bark eaters. (Adirhon 'daks is a Mohawk word meaning "tree eaters.") They ate a variety of green bark from chestnuts, walnut and oak trees. They were particularly fond of the inside bark of the top of the pine, especially during the spring when it was full of sweet sap.

Adirondack Pine Bark Cakes (Traditional)

The inner bark of the Eastern White Pine saved hundreds from starving.

Peel the sweet cambium layer from the white pulp. Dry, then pound into a fine powder. Mix with water to form a thick gruel.

Dig a pit and line with rocks. Make a fire on rocks and burn until rocks become very hot. Mold the thick gruel into large cakes. Remove coals and line rock with green leaves. Place cakes on leaves and cover with a thick layer of green leaves. Rake coals over leaves and cover with damp moss. Let cakes steam one hour.

Place cakes on coal frame and build a smoky fire beneath. Smoke for a week.

When needed, break into bits and boil until soft.

Eastern Pine Tips with Venison (Traditional)

Gather spike-like flower clusters. Cook with chunks of venison or caribou in a pot. Add some dried pumpkin, corn or squash, if on hand.

Algonkin Venison Steak (Modern)

Venison Steaks
Garlic
Melted fat
Mushrooms
Salt and pepper
Watercress

Mince garlic and sprinkle over venison. Brush with fat and grill to desired doneness. Grill mushrooms and serve over steaks. Garnish with watercress.

Apples   Iroquois loved the apple above all other fruits. They were generally eaten raw, but sometimes they were boiled whole or cut up for sauce. The favorite way to cook them, however, was to bake them in ashes. The campfire was brushed aside and the apples laid on a layer of hot, gray ashes; hot embers were raked over these and the fire was rebuilt. Baked apples are called "wada' gonduk."

Bear in a Pit (Traditional)

Dig a pit 2½-ft. wide by 2-ft. deep. Line pit with 8 to 10 layers of green maple or basswood leaves. Lay chunks of bear meat on leaves. Toss in large chunks of pumpkin or squash. Cover with another 8 to 8-10 layers of leaves. Top with stone. Build a fire on top of stones and burn until stones are hot and covered with embers. Mound soil on top and bake for 4 to 5 hours.

Saint Lawrence River Black Duck (Modern)

4 black ducks
¼ lb. fat or oil
6 chopped shallots
5 carrots, cut up
Juniper berries, to taste
Wild cherries, chopped and sweetened

Brown ducks and shallots in large frying pan until all blood is cooked. Pour some fat into roasting pan and put in carrots, juniper and wild cherries. Place birds on top of mixture and roast at 350-degrees F. for 3 hours, basting often with juice in pan.

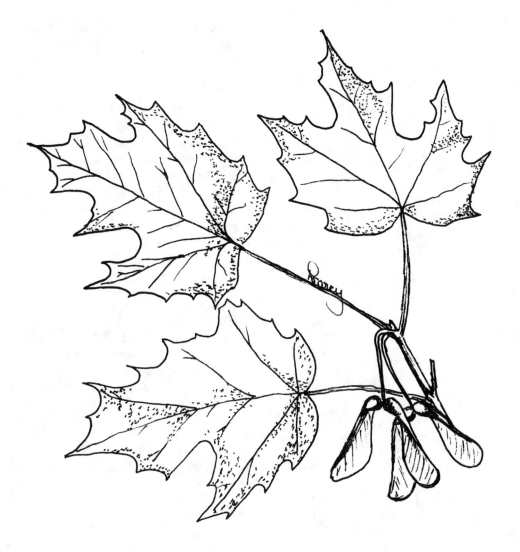

Sugar Maple

Butternut Spread (Traditional)

Gather a quantity of butternuts. Crack nuts and separate meats from shells. Grind nuts to a paste. Traditionally, this was done on a grinding stone, in much the same way as corn was ground. This spread was eaten with bread or corn cakes.

Mushrooms, puffballs, and other edible fungi are esteemed as good materials for soup. The fungus is first peeled, and then diced and thrown into boiling water, seasoned with salt and grease. Sometimes bits of meat were added.

Caribou (Modern)

> **3 lbs. caribou meat**
> **Oil**
> **Onions and carrots**
> **Coarsely ground pepper**
> **Garlic**
> **Flour**
> **Fat**

Marinate meat three or more hours in a mixture of oil, vegetables and pepper. Turn meat regularly so it soaks up marinade. Dry meat and insert pieces of garlic in slits in the meat. Dredge with flour, put in roasting pan and garnish with pieces of fat. Roast at 500-degrees F. for 30 to 35 minutes (rare); 35 to 40 minutes (medium), or 45 minutes to an hour (well-done).

Chestnut Bread (Traditional)

Peel chestnuts and remove inside skin. Pound to a paste. Add enough cornmeal and water to hold together. Form into balls and wrap in green corn shucks, tying each bundle securely. Place in pot of boiling water and cook until done.

The maple tree was regarded by the Iroquois as the goddess of trees and is the only one to which offerings were made. The maple tree started the year. Its returning and rising sap was the sign of the Creator's renewal covenant.

Corn and Nut Pottage with Maple Syrup (Traditional)

Cut sweet corn from the cob and put in kettle along with some dried pumpkin, dried green beans and chopped chestnuts. Cover with water and boil for several hours, adding more water when needed. When ingredients are very soft, add maple syrup to sweeten.

In autumn, when the corn is ripe, when the "great bear chase is on in the heavens," the harvesting begins.

Coal Roasted Corn (Traditional)

Pull husks halfway down ears of corn and remove silk and sprinkle with sea water. Pull husk back over and twist shut. Place over hot coals and turn frequently for about 12 minutes.

"We are the Wavanakis children of the Dawn Country—people of the East. Our lives were spent in hunting and fishing, and our villages were of wigwams. Our garments were of moose hide and fur, our pouches were skins of animals, our dishes were of wood and bark. Tools, knives, tomahawks were stone. With a stone knife, we cut open the moose and with a tool of stone we skinned him. We fished with a bait of stone, greased with moose tallow, on a line of moose sinew. Our lives were simple and glad, and our marriages happy. Man and woman made their vow to the Great Spirit. We believed that Great Spirit, who made all things, is in everything—and that with every breath of air, we drew in the life of the Great Spirit."—Bedagi Spears (Big Thunder)

For cracking nuts, depressions, the size of the nut, were picked into small boulders or slabs of shale. The nut was placed in the depression and cracked with a suitable stone.

95

Hickory Nut-Corn Pudding *(Modern)*

2 eggs
2 Tbsp. maple syrup
2 Tbsp. unbleached flour
1 tsp. salt
2 cups corn, cut from cob
1/2 cup hickory nuts, chopped
2 Tbsp. fat

Pound corn to a mush-like consistency. Mix with remaining ingredients and pour into a baking dish. Bake at 350-degrees F. for 1 hour.

When a youth wishes to marry, he sends wampum to the father of the maid by the hand of one of the old men of the tribe. The old man delivers the wampum and speaks praises of the youth. Should the father send back the wampum to the youth, it is a sign that the suit is rejected. If the wampum is kept, he is accepted.

When the wedding day arrives, the maid and her lover each prepare a great feast. Then a messenger goes through the village, calling, "Your dishes!" This is the signal that the feast begins. All the people gather, men, women and children, bringing bowls and plates.

Hot Coal Squash *(Traditional)*

Put butternut or acorn squash on hot coals, cover with coals and cook 1 1/2 hours, or until a stick can be easily slid into it. Cut in half, remove seeds and serve with maple syrup.

Indian Pudding *(Modern)*

Mix together:
1/4 cup cornmeal
1 cup cold water
1 tsp. salt

Stir in:
2 cups scalded milk

Bring to a boil and cook 10 minutes, stirring. Blend in:

1 egg, well beaten
1/4 cup brown sugar
1/2 cup molasses
1 Tbsp. butter
1 tsp. ground cinnamon
1/2 tsp. ground ginger
1/4 tsp. nutmeg

Pour into buttered, quart-sized casserole and bake 1/2 hour at 300-degrees F. Stir in 1 cup cream.

Bake 2 hours. Serve with ice cream or whipped cream. Good hot or cold.

The Iroquois in pre-colonial and colonial times had one regular meal a day. This was called sedetcinegwa and was eaten between 9 and 11:00 a.m. This did not prevent anyone from eating as often as they wished, for food was always ready in every home at all times.

In the spring, tribes of the Eastern Woodlands move into special maple sugar camps. They tap the trees, collecting the sap on birchbark containers. The sap is poured into wooden troughs and hot stones are dropped into the liquid. It is then worked with wooden paddles until it crystalizes. The sugar is stored for use throughout the year.

Iroquois Expedition Food *(Traditional)*

Dried venison
Dried blueberries, elderberries, blackberries, strawberries
Parched corn
Maple sugar

All ingredients were pounded together with a stone wrapped in rawhide. The pounded ingredients were carried in a parfletch bag or a dried gourd. This food was eaten sparingly with large quantities of water.

Leaf Bread Tamales *(Traditional)*

Cut kernels from green corn and scrape the cob. Beat to a milky paste in mortar. Pat paste into an oblong shape and lay on one end of a broad corn leaf. Double free half of leaf over the paste. Fold other leaves over the first. Tie three times laterally and once transversly with strips of corn husks. Drop in boiling water and cook 45 minutes. Serve with meat drippings. Often, cooked, mashed, red beans are added to the corn before wrapping.

Menominee Venison-Wild Rice Stew *(Modern)*

3½ lbs. venison shoulder, cubed
1½ tsp. salt
2½ quarts wter
Handful of small, wild onions
1½ cups wild rice, rinsed in cold water

Put venison, salt, wild onion and water in large pot. Simmer 1½ hours. Add wild rice and simmer 1½ hours longer.

Micmac Samp *(Traditional)*

Boil coarsely pounded cornmeal in water to form a runny gruel. Add to this dried berries and cooked meat.

Iroquois Fish Soup *(Traditional)*

Boil any type of fish in a quantity of water. Remove bones. Stir in cornmeal to obtain desired consistency. Add wild onions and greens (such as young nettle greens, lamb's quarters, watercress or tender dock leaves).

Iroquois Squirrel Stew *(Modern)*

Salt and pepper squirrels to taste. Boil in water until very tender. Remove meat from bones and save broth. Mix 1 cup cooled cooking broth with flour to make dumpling dough. Put squirrel meat back in broth with 2 Tbsp. butter. Add cut strips of dumpling dough to broth and cook until dumplings are done.

Mohawk Corn *(Modern)*

6 ears of fresh corn
½ cup black walnuts
2 Tbsp. butter

Scrape corn from ears and add to pot along with ½ cup water, walnuts and butter. Heat through.

97

Daniel Gookin, describing Indians in Massachusetts, 1674:

"*Their food is generally boiled maize, mixed with kidney beans...also they frequently boil in this pottage, fish of all sorts, either taken new or dried, as shad, eels, alewives or a kind of herring, cut in pieces, bone and all. I have wondered many times that they were not in danger of being choked with fish bones; but they are so dexterous in separating the bones from the fish in their eating, that they are in no hazard. Also, they boil in this frumenty all sorts of flesh, as venison, beaver, bear, moose, otters, racoons..also, they mix with the said pottages several sorts of roots...*"

Moose Shoulder (*Modern*)

2 lbs. moose shoulder
Minced garlic
Fat
2 to 3 cups moose stock, boiled from bones
Cattail shoots

Cut meat into 1½-inch cubes and brown in fat. Add garlic and cover with stock; simmer on low heat with lid for 2 hours. Add cattail shoots towards end of cooking time.

The axis of the red mulberry leaf contains a milky juice that many tribes use to cure ringworm of the scalp.

Mulberry Cobble (*Modern*)

1 quart ripe mulberries, cleaned and
*   steamed*
½ cup sugar
2 Tbsp. unbleached flour
2 Tbsp. apple cider
1 cup unbleached flour
½ tsp. salt
2 tsp. baking powder
¼ cup lard
½ cup water

Mix berries with sugar and 2 Tbsp. flour. Place into greased casserole or deep dish. Sprinkle with cider.

With fingers, work lard into flour and baking powder. Add water and stir with wooden spoon to form a dough. Roll out on lightly floured board or flat surface. Cover casserole with dough, vent top and bake at 325-degrees F. for 20 minutes.

Ohoⁿ'stä̈ (*Iroquois Dumplings*)

Dumplings are cooked with boiling game birds.

Moisten a mass of cornmeal with boiling water and quickly mold into cakes in the closed hand dampened with cold water. Drop the dumplings, one at a time, into boiling water and boil for a half hour.

Fish the dumplings from the pot with sharpened stick or bone.

Ojibwa Baked Pumpkin (*Modern*)

1 small pumpkin
¼ cup apple cider
¼ cup maple syrup
¼ cup melted butter

Place whole pumpkin in oven and bake at 350 degrees F. for 1½ to 2 hours. Cut hole off top and scoop out pulp and seeds. Set seeds aside for later eating. Mix together remaining ingredients and pour into pumpkin and bake for 35 minutes longer. Cut into wedges and serve.

Ojibwa Corn Cakes (*Modern*)

1¼ cups flour
½ tsp. salt
2 eggs, beaten
1 cup water
2 tsp. melted fat
2½ cups corn, cut from cob

Mix together dry ingredients. Combine eggs, water and fat. Mix into dry ingredients. Stir in corn. Bake on lightly greased griddle.

'Tis the Moon when leaves are falling;
All the wild-rice has been gathered,
And the maize is ripe and ready;
Let us gather in the harvest,
Let us wrestle with Mondamin,
Strip him of his plumes and tassels,
Of his garments green and yellow!"
From The Song of Hiawatha *by H.W. Longfellow*

Oneida Corn Soup *(Traditional)*

Cook corn in water with bits of venison, wild edible greens like cowslip, ferns or milkweed, and a handful of wild rice.

"We always had plenty; our children never cried from hunger, neither were our people in want...the rapids of Rock River furnished us with an abundance of fish, the land being very fertile, never failed to produce good crops of corn, beans, pumpkins and squashes...Here our village stood for more than a hundred years, during all of which time we were the undisputed possessors of the Mississippi valley...If a prophet had come to our village in those days and told us that the things were to take place which have since come to pass, none of our people would have believed him."—Black Hawk, Chief of the Sauk and Fox

Onon' daat *(Mohawk Hominy—Traditional)*

Throw a quart of flint corn in a mortar and moisten with a ladleful of water and a small handful of white ash. Slowly pound with pestle to loosen the hulls. Continue pounding until corn is broken into coarse pieces. Sift corn in a basket so that the hominy passes through and is placed in a bowl while the uncracked corn is thrown back into the mortar and repounded.

The sifted hominy is winnowed so that the lighter chit rises to the surface and is fanned off with the wing of a bird.

The coarse, granular meal is cooked with one part meal and eight parts water. Boil for 2 hours. Add bear meat and beans for flavoring.

Seneca Telling

Hua'tho, the frost spirit, once entered the lodge of the summer spirit O'swi'nodä. A boy, entering the lodge, saw the strange, cold spirit and threw a pot of hot blackberry sauce in the frost spirit's face. Thereafter, Hä' tho never ventured from the north between the time blackberries bloom and the fruit is mature.

Otga asha *(Traditional blackberries)*

Blackberries
Maple sugar
Water

Crush berries. Mix with maple sugar and water to form a sweet gruel.

When picking berries which grow in poisonous, snake infested places, smear your moccasins or boots with lard. The snake, scenting the hog fat, will think that pigs are scouting for them. Rather than risk being eaten, the snakes usually make a hasty retreat.

Yellow Pond Lily Roots were used by numerous tribes in areas in which they were available. The tuberous roots were harvested in the late fall by wading into the marshes and treading them out with the toes. The roots generally grew in five to six feet of water.

Pond Lily Root-Muscrat Stew
(Traditional)

1 cleaned muscrat, cut into serving-sized
pieces
4 to 5 scraped and diced yellow pond lily
tubers
Fistful of wild onions
Grease

Cook muscrat in grease until browned. Add tubers and onions. Cover with water and cook slowly in covered kettle for 6 to 8 hours.

Yellow Pond Lily

Roasted Groundnuts *(Traditional)*

Groundnuts grow from the Maritime Provinces to North Dakota, south to Florida and west to Colorado. The groundnuts lay in strings just beneath the surface and often reach the size of hen's eggs.

Line a pit with stones. The size of the pit depends on the quantity of groundnuts to be roasted. Build a fire on the stones and burn until the stones are hot (3 to 4 hours). Brush away the ashes and lay ground nuts on the stones, single layers. Cover with a heavy layer of wet grass. Shovel dirt over grass, covering well so that steam won't escape.

Steam three hours. Eat hot. Can be rewarmed.

Sassafras Tea *(Traditional)*

8 2-ft. long pieces of sassafras roots
2 quarts water

Scrub roots and rinse. Place in large kettle with water. Slowly bring to boiling, reduce heat and simmer gently for 15 minutes. Remove from heat and let stand 10 minutes. Strain and drink.

"Your forefathers crossed the great waters and landed upon this land. Their numbers were small. They found us friends and not enemies. They told us they had fled from their own country on account of wicked men and had come here to enjoy their religion. They asked for a small seat. We took pity on them and granted their request and they sat down among us. We gave them corn and meat; they gave us poison (rum) in return..."—Red Jacket, Seneca Chief, late 1700s

Seneca Squirrel *(Modern)*

2 large squirrels
Strips of pork fat
Garlic
Carrots

Wrap squirrels in pork fat strips and place in roasting pan with carrots and garlic. Roast at 350-degrees for 1½ hours.

Venison Stew *(Modern)*

Venison, cubed
Onions
Parsley
Carrots
Potatoes
Fat
Salt and pepper
Water

Flour venison and brown in fat. Add onions and brown. Combine venison and onions with carrots, parsley and potatoes and simmer in heavy pot until tender.

"In my youthful days, I have seen large herds of buffalo on these prairies, and elk were found in every grove, but they are here no more, having gone towards the setting sun. For hundreds of miles no white man lived, but now trading posts and settlers are found here and there throughout the country and in a few years the smoke from their cabins will be seen to ascend from every grove, and the prairie covered with their corn fields."—Shabonee, peace chief of the Potawatomi, 1827

Venison and Wild Rice Stew *(Modern)*

3 lbs. venison cubes
2 tsp. salt
2 quarts water
3 juniper berries, crushed
2 onions, quartered
1½ cups wild rice, rinsed

Put venison, salt, water, juniper and onion in kettle. Simmer for 3 hours. Add rice, cover and simmer until rice is tender and most of the liquid has been absorbed.

Wataton guous Odiskwa *(Traditional Popcorn Pudding)*

Pop corn in a clay kettle and then pulverize in a mortar and mix with maple syrup.

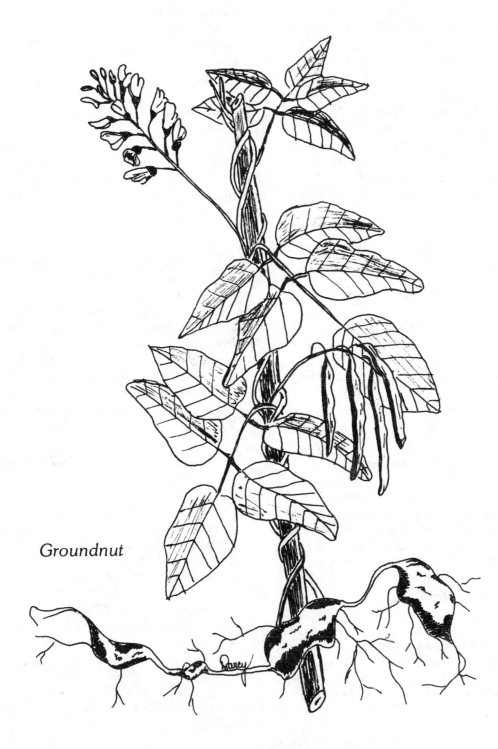

Groundnut

Winter Corn Chowder *(Modern)*

1 1/2 cups dried corn
3 cups broth
6 slices bacon
2 cups chopped onion
4 cups milk
2 tsp. sugar
1/2 tsp. salt

Rinse corn and combine with broth in saucepan; bring to boil. Remove to heat and allow to stand for 2 hours, then cook for 45 minutes.

Cook bacon in skillet until crisp. Drain. Cook onion in drippings. Add to corn mixture and simmer 5 minutes. Add milk, sugar and salt. Sprinkle with bacon.

The nut season to the Iroquois was one of the happiest times of the year, especially for the young who did the work of gathering the crop. The nut season was called o'wadawisa'hõ'.

Winter Squash with Hickory *(Modern)*

1 butternut or acorn squash
2 Tbsp. butter, melted
Dash salt
1/4 cup maple syrup
1/2 cup chopped hickory nuts

Place whole squash in preheated 350-degree F. oven and bake for 35 minutes, or until tender. Cut baked squash in half and scoop out seeds.

Scoop pulp from skin and place pulp in bowl with 1 Tbsp. butter, salt and 1 Tbsp. syrup. Mash until smooth. Fold in nuts and turn into a buttered casserole; smooth surface.

Combine remaining syrup and butter and drizzle over squash. Bake at 450-degrees F. for 20 minutes.

Yellowjacket Soup *(Traditional)*

Large yellow jacket nest filled with grubs

Loosen all uncovered grubs and set aside. Heat the nest with the remaining grubs over fire until paper-like covering parches. Pick out the grubs and brown them over fire with those which had been set aside. Cook the browned grubs in boiling water to make soup. Season with salt.

BIBLIOGRAPHY

American Indian Cooking and Herb Lore, J.E. Sharp and T.B. Underwood, Cherokee Press, 1973

American Indian Food and Lore, Carolyn Niethammer, Collier Macmillan Publ., 1974

Blackfoot Lodge Tales, George Bird Grinnel, University of Nebraska Press, 1962

Edible Plants of the Rocky Mountains, H.D. Harrington, University of New Mexico, 1980

Empire of the Columbia, Harper and Row, 1957

Field Guide to Edible Wild Plants, Bradford Angier, Stockpole Books, 1974

Field Guide to Edible Wild Plants, Lee Peterson, Houghton Mifflin Co., 1977

The Herb Book, John Lust, Bantam Books, 1974

How to Prepare Common Wild Foods, Darcy Williamson, Maverick Publications, 1978

Indians of the Americas, National Geographic Society, 1955

Indian Legends from the Northern Rockies, Ella E. Clark, University of Oklahoma Press, 1966

Indian Masks and Myths of the West, Joseph W. Wherry, Funk and Wagnalls, 1969

Indian Women of the Western Morning, J.U. and D.M. Terrell, Anchor Books, 1976

Indians of the Plains, R.H. Lowis, Natural History Press, 1954

Indians of the Northwest Coast, Philip Ducker, Natural History Press, 1955

The Indian Tipi, Reginald and Gladys Laubin, Ballantine Books, 1957

Nature's Medicines, Richard Luccas, Wilshire Book Co., 1977

NuNee Poom Tit Wah Tit, Nez Pierce Tribe, 1972

Outdoor Survival Skills, Larry Dean Olson, Brigham Young University Press, 1973

Parker on the Iroquois, Wm. N. Fenton, Syracuse University Press, 1968

Skills for Taming the Wilds, Bradford Angier, Stockpole Books, 1967

Stalking the Healthful Herbs, Euell Gibbons, David McKay, 1966

Wild Berries of the Pacific Northwest, J. E. Underhill, Superior Publ. Co., 1974

Wild Foods of the Desert, Darcy Williamson, Maverick Publications, 1986

The Wild Food Trail Guide, Alan Hall, Holt, Rinehart and Winston, 1976

INDEX

Cont'd...from back cover

"Indexing is the most tedious part of the process," she says. "Take Chinook Berry Shortcake. It's got to go under 'C' for Chinook, 'B' for Berry and...well, you get the idea."

The book includes recipes, legends and healing methods from tribes throughout the United States. Both writers agreed the book should have a free-flowing structure, moving from one subject to the next in a natural conversational style.

"There isn't a section on modern cooking and another on traditional," Williamson says. "The recipes are interspersed with bits of legends, like the story of the white fish and the sucker fish and how the sucker fish got all its scales. Then there is a traditional Nez Perce recipe for white fish."

Recipes for some little-known traditional foods, such as *stewed dog*, includes explanations of their significance ("It was a mark of distinction to be served dog," Williamson points out), and the book is liberally sprinkled with Indian philosophies about food, a subject Railsback knows well.

"There's a quote from a Yuman woman, talking about how the food used to be so good and from the land and now there is sickness because they're eating white man's food," she says. "That is followed by a standard modern-day reservation meal, a commodity meal with white flour, sugar, dried eggs, elbow macaroni, all these starchy staples."

Railsback lashes out at what she says reservation food has done to Indians.

"People are always saying, 'Why is the Indian so fat?' Well, it's because of the diet," she says. "Look at old pictures of the Indian people and you'll see they were all lean. They were very healthy and lived to way into their 100s. Nowadays about all you can do with that commodity food is gain weight on it."

Indian natural healing methods are included in the book, but not as a separate section. A recipe for frying prickly pear cactus, for example, is followed with instructions on the preparation and use of the cactus gum as a salve. Railsback believes it's important to explain when and how to pick medicinal plants to get the most benefit from them.

"There were recipes for teas, handed down through the ages by the medicine people," she says. "Let's say that an Indian wanted clover tops. The clover is a sun plant, so he goes during the day, about 11 o'clock when the sap is in the flower."

"First he looks for the chief plant or the mother plant and pretty soon it will make itself known to him. Maybe it is the biggest or the most beautiful; maybe not, but he will know. And he goes to this plant and says 'I won't harm you and I'll take only what I need from you,' and gives the plant something in exchange."

She says there is food value or healing properties in just about every wild plant, although white Americans see most wild plants as weeds.

"It's called a weed because it won't live peaceably among the garden plants, with their water and fertilizer," Williamson says.

"To an Indian there's no such thing as a weed," Railsback adds, then grins.

by Alice Koskela
for the *Lewiston Morning Tribune*